Contents

HISTORY OF THE TOPKAPI PALACE MUSEUM

Topkapı Palace was not only the residence of the Ottoman sultans, but also the administrative and educational centre of the state. Initially constructed between 1460 and 1478 by Sultan Mehmed II, the conqueror of Constantinople, and expanded upon and altered many times throughout its long history, the palace served as the home of the Ottoman sultans and their court until the middle of the 19th century. In the early 1850s, the palace became inadequate to the requirements of state ceremonies and protocol, and so the sultans moved to Dolmabahçe Palace, located on the Bosphorus. Despite this move, the royal treasure, the Holy Relics of the Prophet Muhammad, and the imperial archives continued to be preserved at Topkapı, and-since the palace was the ancestral residence of the Ottoman dynasty as well as the place where the Holy Relics were preserved-Topkapı continued to play host to certain state ceremonies. Following the abolishment of the Ottoman monarchy in 1922, Topkapı Palace was converted into a museum on April 3rd 1924, on the order of Mustafa Kemal Atatürk.

After the conquest of Constantinople, Sultan Mehmed II (r. 1444-46, 1451-81) had a palace built in what is modern-day Istanbul's Beyazıt district, on the spot where the University of Istanbul stands today; this first palace subsequently became known as the Old Palace (Eski Saray). Following the construction of the Old Palace, Mehmed II then had the Tiled Kiosk (Çinili Köşk) built, followed by Topkapı Palace itself, to which the court relocated when construction was complete. Mehmed called this place the New Palace (Sarây-ı Cedîd). The palace received its current name when Sultan Mahmud I (r. 1730-54) had a large wooden palace constructed near the city's Byzantine walls, in front of which were placed several ceremonial cannons. This seaside palace was named the Cannon Gate Palace by the Sea (Topkapusu Sâhil Sarâyı), and when this palace was destroyed in a fire, its name was transferred to Mehmed II's New Palace.

Topkapı Palace, which developed and grew over the centuries, had a design that played an important role in Ottoman governmental philosophy and in the relations between the palace and its subjects. When Topkapı was first built, its plan was influenced by the splendor of the Edirne Palace located on the Tunca River, which had been constructed by Mehmed II's father, Sultan Murad II (r. 1421-44, 1446-51) but very little of which survives today. The basic design of the palace is centred on various courtyards and gardens, around which are arranged offices devoted to state business, the buildings and pavilions serving as the residence of the sovereign and the buildings set aside for the court employees who lived in the palace.

Topkapı Palace is built atop the Byzantine acropolis on Sarayburnu at the tip of the Istanbul peninsula. It is surrounded by the Sea of Marmara, the Bosphorus and the Golden Horn. On the land side, the palace is surrounded by 1,400-meter-long high encircling walls-known as the "Royal Walls" (Sûr-ı Sultânî)-while on the side facing the sea it is surrounded by Byzantine walls. The palace covers an area of approximately 700,000 square meters, a major part of which area is set aside for the Royal Gardens (Hasbahçe). The court of Topkapı Palace proper is made up of two basic organizations: the Outer Palace (Bîrûn) and the Inner Palace (Enderûn); the Harem was a part of the latter. The design of residences, ceremonies and ceremonial spaces, and all of the many palace facilities were set out according to this basic organizational principle.

Within the Topkapı Palace complex are three main gates-the Imperial Gate (Bâb-ı Hümâyûn), the Gate of Salutation (Bâbüsselâm), and the Gate of Felicity (Bâbüssaâde)-four courtyards, the Harem, the Royal Gardens-today known as the Rose Garden (Gülbahçe)-and various other gardens.

Inscriptions over the Imperial Gate

The Imperial Gate
(Bâb-ı Hümâyûn)

This gate, built as the main entrance on the palace's Hagia Sophia side in the time of Sultan Mehmed II (the Conqueror), bears above it an inscription in Arabic by `Ali ibn Yahya as-Sufi, which reads as follows: "By the grace and assent of God and with the aim of establishing peace and tranquility. This auspicious citadel was built and erected in the blessed month of Ramadan in the year 883 [November-December 1478] at the command of the son of Sultan Murad, son of Sultan Mehmed Khan, the sultan of the lands and the emperor of the seas, the shadow of God extending over men and djinn, the deputy of God in the East and in the West, the champion of the water and the land, the conqueror of Constantinople and father of that conquest Sultan Mehmed, may God make his reign eternal and exalt his abode above that of the highest stars in the firmament."

Above the Imperial Gate, verses 45-48 of the Qur'an's Surah al-Hijr are inscribed in müsennâ ("doubled") script, in which the writing is "mirrored". This inscription is important both in terms of the beauty of its calligraphy and in terms of the significance of the verses-which read, in part, "Enter in peace and security!" (udkhuluha bisalamin aminina)-to the Ottoman conception of royalty. On the other side of the gate, just above the calligraphic seal (tuğra) of Sultan Abdülaziz (r. 1861-76), is inscribed a portion of verse 13 of Surah as-Saff: "Help from God and a speedy victory. Give thou good tidings [O Muhammad] to the believers!" (nasrun min Allahi wa fathun qaribun wa bashshiri al-mumina); this was also the verse recited by the Janissary marching band (mehterân) prior to a charge.

The Imperial Gate underwent frequent alterations over the years and in old prints a small pavilion is visible above the gate. This pavilion was used for the observance of processions and the safekeeping of inheritances, but was destroyed by fire in the year 1865.

An Anonymous engraving of the Imperial Gate

A recent photograph of the Imperial Gate

The Imperial Gate and the Fountain of Ahmed III at the beginning of the 20th century

THE FIRST COURTYARD

The First Courtyard is reached through the Imperial Gate. This courtyard, where various ceremonies and processions were held, was the only part of the palace open to the public. The Deâvî Pavilion, of which only the foundation has survived to the present day, was located near the Gate of Salutation (Bâbüsselâm or "Middle Gate") and was where the public conveyed their written petitions to the palace.

On the left side of the courtyard stand the church of Hagia Eirene (Aya İrini) and the Royal Mint (Darphâne-i Âmire). It was also here that the Firewood Storehouse, the Wickerworkers' Headquarters, and the Patriarchate were located; the remains of the latter can be seen behind the administrative building and sentry station which were built at the end of the 19th century. On the right side of the courtyard stood the Ministry of Finance; the Palace Hospital; bakeries producing bread and simit for the palace; the Mosque of the Royal Bakery; and employees' residences. There was also a water tower that contained a fountain and was built in the time of Sultan Mahmud II (r. 1808-39). One of the most interesting structures remaining in the First Courtyard is the Executioners' Fountain, which can be seen on the right of the Gate of Salutation; here, purportedly, executioners would wash their hands following an execution. It was also in this area of the courtyard that the palace woodsheds were located.

In this courtyard, there are two small gates opening onto the Royal Garden: on the Golden Horn side is the Kozbekçileri Gate; on the Sea of Marmara side is the Gate of the Boot. The most important and oldest structure in the courtyard is the Byzantine church of Hagia Eirene, built in the 6th century to serve as the church for the Patriarchate. Following the construction of Topkapı Palace, Hagia Eirene was used as an armory. Later, during the time of Fethi Ahmed Pasha (1802-58), it was converted into the Archaeology Museum, serving in this capacity until 1894, when the Archaeology Museum

△ *The Church of Saint Eirene*

◁ *Miniature depicting the enthronement of Süleyman I in 1520 in the First Courtyard. (Süleymannâme)*

was moved to the building it currently occupies and Hagia Eirene became a military museum.

When the court moved out of Topkapı Palace in the 19th century the palace workshops where fine arts were carried out, were initially converted into the Royal Mint where imperial coins were pressed.

The First Courtyard (Alay Meydanı)

The Second Courtyard (Council Square)
  A. The Imperial Stables Court
  1. The Gate of Salutation (Bâbüsselâm) / Middle Gate
  2. The Imperial Kitchens
  3. The Helvahâne
  4. The Şerbethâne
  5. The Dormitory of Cooks
  6. Court of the Kitchens
  7. The Gate of Stables
  8. The Beşir Ağa Mosque
  9. The Imperial Stables
  10. The Dormitory of the Halberdiers with Tresses
  11. The Tower of Justice (Kasrı-ı Adl)
  12. The Harem Gate
  13. The Domed Chamber (Kubbealtı) / The Imperial Council
  14. The Old Treasury (External Treasury)
  15. The Gate of Felicity (Bâbüssaâde)

Third Courtyard (Enderun Courtyard)
  16. The Audience Chamber
  17. The Library of Sultan Ahmed III
  18. The Dormitory of the Campaigners (Seferli Koğuşu)
  19. The Conqueror's Pavilion (The Enderun Treasury)
  20. The Corps of Pantry Keepers (Kilerli Koğuşu)
  21. The Dormitory of the Treasury
  22. The Treasury of the Chamberlain (Silahdar Hazinesi)
  23. Privy Room / Building Housing the Holy Relics
  24. The Privy Room Dignitaries
  25. The Enderun Ağalar Mosque
  26. The Aviary and the Harem Gate

The Harem
  B. The Courtyard of the Black Harem Eunuchs
  C. The Courtyard of Concubines
  D. The Courtyard of the Queen Mother (Valide Sultan)
  E. The Courtyard of the Harem Hospital
  F. The Harem Garden
  G. Gardens
  I. Pool
  J. The Chamberlain's Courtyard

The Fourth Courtyard
  H. Garden
  K. Garden
  27. The Chamber of Clothes
  28. The Revan Kiosk
  29. The Circumcision Chamber
  30. The Fast Breaking Pergola
  31. The Baghdad Kiosk
  32. Sofa Kiosk (Kara Mustafa Pasha Kiosk)
  33. The Chamber of the Chief-Physician
  34. The Mecidiye Kiosk

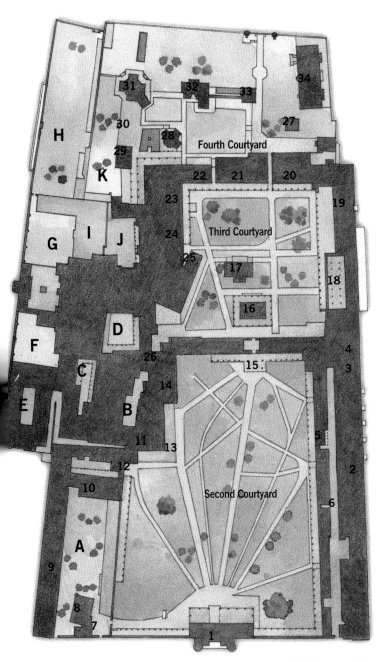

Fourth Courtyard

Third Courtyard

Second Courtyard

0 5 10 15 20 25   50m

THE SECOND COURTYARD

The Gate of Salutation (Bâbüsselâm), also known as the Middle Gate (Orta Kapı) leads into the palace proper. With its two grand towers, it served as a symbol of the pomp and majesty of the Ottoman state and has since become an icon for the whole of Topkapı Palace as well. Built during the reign of Sultan Mehmed II, the Gate of Salutation subsequently underwent numerous renovations in the 16th and 17th centuries. According to one inscription on the gate, the large iron door was made by İsa bin Mehmed in 1524 and an additional inscription states that the gate underwent restoration in 1758. On the upper part of the gate, there is a beautiful calligraphic inscription of the Muslim profession of faith: "There is no god but God; Muhammad is the prophet of God" (La ilaha illallah Muhammadu'r-rasulullah). Only the sultan was allowed to pass through the Gate of Salutation on horseback; the grand vizier and all other state officials were required to dismount before entering. However, the women of the palace were allowed to go through the gate in royal carriages.

The Gate of Salutation's two towers were constructed in the time of Sultan Suleiman I (r. 1520-66), known in English as Suleiman the Magnificent and in Turkish as Suleiman the Lawgiver (Kanûnî). The museum visit currently begins at the Gate of Salutation.

The Second Courtyard, also known as the Council

An engraving depicting the Second Courtyard of the Topkapı Palace by Antoine-Ignace Melling

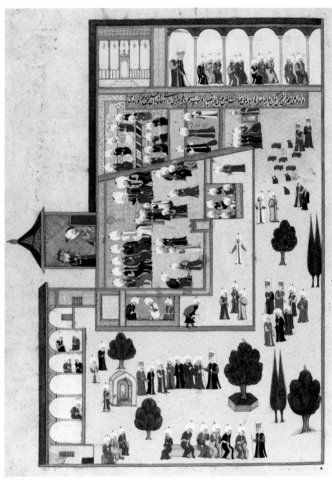

Miniature depicting a court meeting taking place at the Domed Chamber and the Second Courtyard. (Hünernâme)

Square (Dîvân Meydanı), was laid out in the 1460s shortly after Sultan Mehmed II had conquered the city. It served as an official representation of the Ottoman state, being a ceremonial grounds for state governance. Here were held the ceremonies of royal enthronement (cülûs-ı hümâyûn), formal holiday festivities, the reception of ambassadors, and the stipend paid to the sultan's household soldiers (`ulûfe dîvânı), among them the Janissary corps. On the right side of the courtyard, behind the portico, are the palace kitchens. On the left side stand the Tower of Justice and the Domed Chamber (Kubbealtı); the latter is where meetings of the Imperial Council (Dîvân-ı Hümâyûn) were held. Near the Domed

△ Ceiling
  decorations of
  Gate of Salutation.
  (Bâbüsselâm)

◁ The Gate of
  Salutation.
  (Bâbüsselâm)

Entrance of the Domed Chamber

Chamber stands the External Treasury, currently home to the museum's weapons collection. In this corner of the courtyard is the Carriage Gate leading to the Harem apartments can also be seen.

In the courtyard to the left of the Gate of Salutation are two fountains constructed in the time of Sultan Ahmed III (r. 1703-30), while to the right of the gate are an open-air prayer ground (namazgâh) from the time of Sultan Selim III (r. 1789-1807) and large fragments of columns dating back to the Byzantine era. Also noteworthy in this courtyard are the Byzantine cisterns-located on the Sultan's Way. The Sultan's Way leads through the Gate of Salutation to the Gate of Felicity (Bâbüssaâde). On the Viziers' Way, which leads to the Domed Chamber, salutation stones mark where dignitaries would stop to perform their salutations.

The Domed Chamber (Kubbealtı) and The Imperial Council (Dîvân-ı Hümâyûn)

On the edge of the Second Courtyard stands the Domed Chamber which in a sense represents the universal nature of the Ottoman Empire. The rather modest three-dome space of the current Domed Chamber, from which the empire was governed for a good portion of its history, was constructed in the 16th century on the order of Suleiman the Magnificent as a replacement for the wooden council chamber that had been built together with the original palace. The building was seriously damaged in the Harem fire of 1665, and as a result it had to be rebuilt almost entirely. It was rebuilt during the reign of Sultan Mehmed IV (r. 1648-87). Inscriptions on the Domed Chamber's outer façade state that the building underwent various restorations in later times as well.

Interior of the Domed Chamber

The area from where clerks followed the deliberations at the Imperial Council

An engraving depicting the entrance of the Grand Vizier into the Domed Chamber by Thomas Allom

The face of the Domed Chamber looks onto the courtyard and is surrounded by a wide portico consisting of eleven columns of green porphyry and white marble. The portico's arches support a wooden roof adorned with splendid engraved decorations.

Meetings of the Imperial Council would occur four times a week at the Domed Chamber located beneath the Tower of Justice (Kasr-ı Adl). The adjacent domed space served as the office of the Imperial Council's secretary, while the last room served as the Imperial Archives (Defterhâne).

Though an Imperial Council under the leadership of the Ottoman sovereign had met ever since the empire was established, sultans ceased to chair the council's meetings personally in the time of Sultan Mehmed II. Instead, they would simply follow the proceedings by sitting in a small room separated from the meeting

The ceiling ornamentations of the Imperial Council

View of the grille from which the sultan followed the deliberations

chamber by a grille. They would, however, signal when the proceedings were at an end, either by striking the grille with their scepter or, more rarely, by means of an oral announcement. The resolutions made by the Imperial Council were recorded in the Registries of Important Events (Mühimme Defterleri).

The place of referral for the Imperial Council was the Audience Chamber (Arz Odası), located just inside the Gate of Felicity. On days appointed for the reception of petitions, after the meeting in the Domed Chamber had concluded, the viziers would come here at appointed times and present formal written proposals (lâyiha) to the grand vizier.

The Tower of Justice
(Kasr-ı Adl)

Visible from much of Istanbul, the Tower of Justice symbolizes the grandness and majesty of the Ottoman Empire. The tower is, in fact, tall enough to bear comparison even with the minarets of such monumental structures as Hagia Sophia and the Mosque of Sultan Ahmed (the "Blue Mosque"). The tower was built during the reign of Sultan Mehmed II as a symbol of the imperial court. Following the 1665 fire in the palace, the tower was rebuilt in stone. Similar towers were ubiquitous in Ottoman palaces, such as those at the Han Palace in Bahçesaray and at the Edirne Palace. During the 18th century, similar towers could even be found at the mansions of some of the landed gentry.

The sultan would enter the Tower of Justice from the Harem and proceed to a small room from which he would listen in on the meetings of the Imperial Council. The council members were well aware of his hidden presence behind the grille that separated the Domed Chamber from this room in the Tower of Justice, and so would take care to conduct the proceedings with the highest degree of seriousness and discipline. The Tower of Justice takes its name from this supervisory activity of the sultan. The top floor of the Tower of Justice (which was also known as the Royal Tower (Kasr-ı Sultânî)) afforded a wide view of the palace's environs and as a result, was used to monitor the development and progress of revolts and to observe the surrounding area.

View of the Harem Roof

The External Treasury

Built during the reign of Sultan Suleiman the Magnificent, the eight-domed External Treasury (located adjacent to the Domed Chamber) served as the official imperial treasury. The great quantities of gold and silver, stored in large jars in the treasury, were the impetus behind numerous "internal affairs" that transpired in the empire's last years. Much of the money and valuables constituting the empire's expenditures were stored here, among them the stipend paid to the sultan's household soldiers once every three months (ulûfe dîvânı); the special money and valuables (known as surre-i hümâyûn) sent to the holy sites in Mecca and Medina (haremeyn-i şerîfeyn); and the money distributed when a new sultan was enthroned (cülûs bahşîşi).

Currently, the External Treasury houses the museum's weapons collection.

Palace Kitchen. (Matbah-ı Âmire)

The Tressed Halberdiers (Zülüflü Baltacılar)

Consisting both of servants used to provide general services to the palace and the Harem, and of soldiers forming a part of the sultan's household troop, the halberdiers and axmen were a rather important part of the organization of the Inner Palace (Enderûn). It is believed that, during military campaigns, these soldiers would advance before the main body of the army in order to fell any trees that might hinder the army's advance. The navy blue vests, called dolama, of the Tressed Halberdiers bore collars high enough to obstruct the wearer's sight on both sides, preventing him from seeing his surroundings while working inside the Harem. The halberdiers were called "tressed" owing to the two side locks of hair hanging down from beneath their headdresses.

The Tressed Halberdiers had several duties. Among them were the provision of firewood to the Harem, carrying the sultan's throne to and from the Gate of Felicity whenever required and the guarding and maintaining the chambers of the Imperial Council. During battle, the Tressed Halberdiers would continuously recite the Qur'an under their regimental colours so as to ensure victory for the army.

The Halberdiers' Barracks is among the palace's oldest buildings. They were accessed through a door located to the right of the Carriage Gate leading to the Harem apartments. Built around a courtyard in a style typical of traditional Turkish residential architecture, the barracks' ceramic tiled walls and finely embellished woodwork are especially noteworthy. The barracks were first constructed in the 15th century and formed a single complex with its own bath and small mosque whose mihrab (or niche indicating the direction of the Kaaba in Mecca) is adorned with coloured Iznik tiles. The barracks' Pipe Room was used by the halberdiers for relaxation. The barracks were where the halberdiers would sleep, and had two storeys: novice halberdiers would sleep on the lower floor, veterans on the upper floor.

The Imperial Stables (Istabl-ı Âmire)

The Imperial Stables begin beside the Beşir Ağa Mosque and extend as far as the Halberdiers' Barracks. They were used to keep the horses belonging to the sultan and to officials of the Inner Palace. In the single-domed space on the building's north side, as well as in the adjacent rooms, was kept the Treasury of the Royal Tack (Raht-ı Hümâyûn, Raht Hazînesi), the riding equipment used by the sultan. Gold and silver saddles, riding crops, stirrups, bits, and bridles, all decorated with jewelry, would be registered in the records of this treasury, affixed with the Royal Seal (Mühr-i Hümâyûn), and stored here. This structure also contained the offices of the Chief Stable Steward (Baş İmrahor) and the other stable managers. The section of the stable containing the horse stalls is long and narrow. The inscription above the stable door states that, in 1736, the stable underwent restoration, while the mosque and bathhouse on the courtyard were rebuilt. The watering troughs found in the courtyard date back to the reigns of Sultan Mehmed II and Sultan Murad III.

The current appearance of the Imperial Stables dates back to the restoration carried out in 1939-42. The ceiling of the Chief Stable Steward's office was placed here in 1942 having been brought from the Köçeoğlu mansion in the Bebek neighborhood of Istanbul. The stables are currently used to house temporary exhibitions.

The Beşir Ağa Mosque

Located on the road leading to the gate of the Imperial Stables, the Beşir Ağa Mosque was built for use as a prayer room for stable employees by Hacı Beşir Agha, the keeper of the Abode of Felicity (Dârüssaâde) or Harem in the time of Sultan Mahmud I (r. 1730-54). Beşir Ağa also had a fountain and bathhouse built beside the mosque; the bathhouse, known as the Halberdiers' Bathhouse remained in use up to the 1920s, but unfortunately the building has not survived. The mosque and bathhouse primarily served employees of the Outer Palace, mainly seeing use by those working in the Imperial Stables and those residing in the Halberdiers' Barracks.

The Imperial Kitchens (Matbah-ı Âmire)

Serving the Ottoman royal family as well as the thousands of palace employees, the Imperial Kitchens were first built in the time of Sultan Mehmed II (r. 1451-81) and subsequently expanded by Sultan Suleiman the Magnificent (r. 1520-66) to respond to the increase in the population of the palace. Following the fire of 1574, the kitchens were repaired and restructured by the architect Sinan. The roof of the Imperial Kitchens consists of ten domes and ten spires. Currently, the kitchens are used to display Ottoman kitchen utensils and other artifacts related to the cuisine of the palace.

There are three doors along the long portico of the kitchen section. The first one opens to the Imperial Pantry (Kilâr-ı Amire), the second one to the Royal Kitchen, and the third one to the Confectionery House (Helvâhâne).

As a precautionary measure against any assassination attempts on the sultan, the food prepared in the Imperial Kitchens was first tested by the cooks and then by the royal taster (çâşnîgîr). Some sixty types of food were typically served to the sultan, and as a matter of course, he did not eat them all: some he would only look at, while others he would merely taste, and whatever was left over would be given to other dignitaries to eat, according to the protocol. This process was, in fact, a very old tradition in the East as well as among the Turks.

DESSERTS OF THE PALACE

In the final division of the Imperial Kitchens, the Confectionery House, there was an entire company of workers including six master chefs and up to one hundred apprentices whose sole duty was to prepare candies, halva, pastries, and syrups. In the winter, they would make the gumlike candy called "macun" by using sugars and flavours obtained from roses, musk, poppies, galangal root (Alpinia officinarum), Indonesian long peppers (Piper longum), and various other spices. The "macun" thus prepared would then be offered to the sultan, the members of the Imperial Council, and the officials of the Inner Palace. Perhaps the most famous confections prepared in this kitchen were lokma (a fried-dough pastry soaked in syrup or honey and cinnamon) and Noah's pudding, known as "aşure" in Turkish. During Muharram, the first month in the Islamic calendar, aşure with honey, sugar, and strained musk would be prepared with the latter being made especially for the sultan and the inhabitants of the Harem.

Ottoman cuisine developed into one of the richest and most unique of all palace cuisines largely as a result of the Imperial Kitchens having the need to prepare food for such a large palace population in addition to distributing it to those in the immediate environs of the palace.

The chimneys of the Palace Kitchens as viewed from the Second Courtyard

THE SULTAN DINED ALONE

The statutes of laws (kanûnnâme) set forth by Sultan Mehmed II between 1477 and 1481, in addition to establishing the foundations of the Ottoman Empire's administrative, legal, penal, fiscal, and military organization, also determined the rules for table manners. Prior to this, sultans not only used to dine together with their viziers but were also required to eat a ceremonial meal in the presence of their troops. At the beginning of his reign, Mehmed II is known to have dined together with his scholars; however, in his statute of laws, he abolished the custom of the sultan's eating in the presence of others. This rule was strictly adhered to until the time of Sultan Abdülaziz (r. 1861-76), who once dined together with the Crown Prince Edward (VII) of the United Kingdom.

Various explanations have been offered as to why Mehmed II established this rule, among them the arguments that he thought no one worthy of sharing his company, that he feared being poisoned, and that one of the scholars with whom he had used to dine had raised an argument as to who should sit to the sultan's right and who to his left. But whatever the reason for the decision, it certainly has had important consequences for historians as the items on the sultan's personal menu can only be inferred from the account ledgers of the Imperial Kitchens. Judging from these ledgers alone, it appears that Mehmed II's personal preferences included caviar, roe, shrimp and oysters.

However, there are more extensive records of the food served to ambassadors, which can be seen in ambassadorial records and travel accounts. Among the dishes served at the banquets given to ambassadors were lamb and chicken kebabs, pigeons roasted in butter, various soups, various types of "börek" (a type of unsweetened baked or fried filled pastry) and pilaf, vegetable stews, milk puddings and sweet pastries. As dessert, the filo-based baklava (which was created in the Imperial Kitchens by means of a refinement of the layered doughs of Central Asian tradition) was also common. At the end of the meal sherbet was served. Sherbet is an aromatic cooled beverage prepared by combining honey- or sugar-sweetened ice with the fragrant petals of roses, violets, oranges, lemons, and jasmine, sometimes with the addition of verjuice to impart a slightly sour flavour. The snow and ice used in the preparation of sherbet was provided by the city's merchants, who brought it in from the mountains around Mudanya and Bursa.

Olive oil-based dishes such as "imambayıldı" (braised eggplant stuffed with onion, garlic, and tomatoes) and "dolma" were products of the second half of the 18th century at the earliest. Prior to this, Turks did not consume olive oil as food, preferring suet or butter instead.

The Byzantine Water Cistern

As all great civilizations must, the Ottomans attributed great importance to water and there are still traces of Ottoman water culture at the Topkapı Palace. In Byzantine times, the Sarayburnu district in which the palace was built boasted more than forty cisterns, channels and wells. One of these is the Byzantine cistern located on the Sultan's Way leading to the Gate of Felicity which is thought to date back to the 5th century.

The Sukhumi Fortress Monument

This monument, located in the Second Courtyard near the Gate of Felicity, consists of the inscription panel commemorating the construction by Sultan Ahmed III (r. 1703-30) of the fortress built in Sukhumi, a city located in Abkhazia on the eastern coast of the Black Sea. The monument bears the calligraphic seal (tuğra) of Sultan Abdülhamid II (r.1876-1909) who had the panel removed from the fortress at the close of the Russo-Turkish War of 1877-78 when it became clear that the Ottomans were going to lose the fortress. The monument was erected here to serve as an object lesson for all.

The Gate of Felicity (Bâbüssaâde)

The Gate of Felicity, whose imposing appearance symbolizes the sovereignty of the Ottoman Empire and its ruler, served as the entrance to the private residence of the sultan. Also known as the Gate of the White Eunuchs (Akağalar Kapısı), it was first constructed on the order of Sultan Mehmed II and was originally fronted by four columns; these were later removed and the shape of the gate was changed (an inscription above the gate's arch commemorates its restoration in 1774). At the very top, in the calligraphic

---

▷ *The Gate of Felicity. (Bâbüssaâde)*

▽ *Sultan Selim III's Religious Holiday Ceremony. Attributed to Konstantin Kapıdağlı, c. 1789*

THE ENGLISH AMBASSADOR EDWARD BARTON AT THE COURT OF SULTAN MURAD III, 1593

The ambassador thus honourably accompanied, the Chauses foremost, next his men on foote all going by two and two, himselfe last with his Chause and Drugaman or Interpreter and 4 Janisaries, which he doeth usually entertaine in his house to accompany him continually abroad, came to the Seraglio about an English mile from the water side, where first hee passed a great gate into a large court (much like the space before Whitehall gate) where he with his gentlemen alighted and left their horses. From hence they passed into another stately court, being about 6 score in bredth and some 10 score yards long, with many trees in it; where all the court was with great pompe set in order to entertaine our ambassador. Upon the right hand, all the length of the court was a gallerie arched over, and borne up with stone pillars, much like the Roiall Exchange, where stood most of his [the sultan's] guard in rankes from the one end to the other in costly array, with round head pieces on their heads of metall and gilt over, with a great plume of fethers somewhat like a long brush standing up before. On the left hand stood the Cappagies or porters and the Chauses. All these courtiers being about the number of 2000 (as I might well gesse), most of them apparelled in clothe of gold, silver, velvet, sattin and scarlet, did together with bowing their bodies, laying their heads upon their brests in courteous maner of salutation, entertain the Ambassador who likewise passing between them & turning himselfe sometime to the right hand and sometime to the left answered them with the like.

(Rosedale, Rev. H.G., ed. Queen Elizabeth and the Levant Company: A Diplomatic and Literary Episode of the Establishment of Our Trade with Turkey. London: Henry Frowde, 1904. p.11-12)

hand of Sultan Mahmud II (r. 1808-39), is the Arabic formula called the "Basmala" reading 'bismi-llahi'r-rahmani'r-rahim' ("In the name of God, the Merciful, the Compassionate"). The calligraphic seal carved into the arch's keystone belongs to the same sultan, and was inscribed by the calligrapher Rakım Efendi. The raised inscriptions found on both sides of the gate are panegyric for Sultan Abdülhamid I (r. 1774-89). The Gate of Felicity also boasts splendid carved decorations.

The Gate of Felicity has two sets of doors with a short passage between them. In this passage are two additional doors: the one on the right leads to the offices of the Chief of the White Eunuchs (also called the Chief of the Gate of Felicity (Bâbüssaâde Ağası)), while the one on the left leads to the White Eunuchs' Barracks (Akağalar Koğuşu).

The Gate of Felicity would be kept open throughout the day. However, as the gate was not only a symbol of the sultanate and the caliphate but also the entrance to the sultan's private residence, it would by no means be used lightly. The Ottoman throne would be placed before the Gate of Felicity for enthronement ceremonies, the paying of homage to the sultan, and formal holiday festivities. It would also be placed there in times of revolt or discontent, when the Janissaries would be admitted into the Second Courtyard to be received by the sultan.

THE THIRD COURTYARD

The Third Courtyard
(The Inner Palace /
Enderûn Courtyard) is like
the keep of a castle: when
the gates to this courtyard
(surrounded by strong
structures) are shut, entry
is virtually impossible. The
courtyard covers an area
of approximately nine
"dönüm" (decares), with
one "dönüm" (decare)
equaling roughly 920
square meters.

Upon entering the
courtyard from the Gate of
Felicity, the first building
one sees is the Audience
Chamber (Arz Odası)
stood at the centre of the
courtyard. This is where
the sultan received the
grand vizier, other viziers,
and ambassadors. Located
immediately behind the

△ *The Conqueror's Pavillion*

▽ *The Campaigner Corps and
the Chamberlains of the
Inner Palace*

ENDERUN (THE INNER PALACE)

At Topkapı, the Enderûn-which means "the Inner Palace" in Persian-began at the Gate of Felicity. It consisted of the residences of the sultan, the white eunuchs in his service, and other court dignitaries in addition to the various dormitories and barracks around the courtyard, where court education was carried out.

The Library of Sultan Ahmed III and Fountain at The Enderun Courtyard

Third Courtyard. (The Enderun Courtyard)

Audience Chamber is the Library of Sultan Ahmed III which stands like an elegant jewel box in the midst of this grand space. On the right side of the courtyard are the Inner Palace School (Enderûn Mektebi), the Campaigners' Barracks, the Conqueror's Pavillion (Fâtih Köşkü) and the remains of a bathhouse dating to the time of Sultan Selim II (r. 1566-74). On the left side of the Inner Palace Courtyard are the Privy Room (Has Oda), which houses the Holy Mantle of the Prophet (Hırka-i Saâdet) and other holy relics; the Privy Room Dormitory; and the Mosque of the Aghas of the Inner Palace. On the two sides of the Gate of Felicity are located the Greater and the Lesser Chambers of the Inner Palace, the White Eunuchs' Dormitory, and the Apiary. Opposite the gate and across the courtyard, are the Treasury of the Chamberlain, the Dormitory of the Treasury and the Butlers' Dormitory.

The Audience Chamber (Arz Odası)

The Audience Chamber was where the grand vizier would come to present the sultan with the decrees adopted by the Imperial Council. It was first built on the order of Sultan Mehmed II in the 15th century as a place for formal audience. Its basic current appearance dates back to the 16th century, when it was repaired by Sultan Suleiman the Magnificent after having been destroyed in the earthquake of 1509. The Audience Chamber underwent numerous other restorations through the centuries, until, in the time of Sultan Abdülmecid (r. 1839-61), it was severely burnt in a fire with only the divan and the bronze-plated fireplace surviving. Subsequent restorations, including the radical changes introduced in 1946, have resulted in space whose decorations are a far cry from their former grandeur.

While the Audience Chamber was where the sultan and the grand vizier would deliberate over the decisions of the Imperial Council, it was also a space for the reception of state officials, ambassadors, and religious scholars.

The Audience Chamber has three doors: two open towards the Gate of Felicity, while the third opens onto the Inner Palace Courtyard. These were termed the Door of Petitions (Marûzât Kapısı), the Door of Offering (Pîşkeş Kapısı), and the Door of the Sovereign (Hükümdâr Kapısı). Anyone who wished to make a petition to the sultan would enter through the Door of Petitions. Between this door and the Door of Offering

is situated a large window; any gifts brought by foreign ambassadors would be left before this window, later to be taken into the Audience Chamber through the Door of Offering. While the Door of Petitions and the Door of Offering are flush with the ground, the Door of the Sovereign at the back of the structure has steps leading down to the Inner Palace Courtyard. The Gate of Felicity is situated at the highest point of the Sarayburnu area.

The façade of the Audience Chamber is decorated with magnificent ceramic tile panels. The chamber's interior is conspicuous for its numerous elements demonstrating the absolute authority of the sultan. Directly opposite the two front entrances stands the sultan's baldachin-style throne, beside which is a fireplace. There is also a fountain inside

The Audience Chamber

the Audience Chamber, mirroring the one that stands outside.

The throne, with its four wreathed columns, dates back to the time of Sultan Mehmed III (r. 1595-1603). The splendid dome supported by these columns is decorated with lacquered animal and floral motifs, in the interstices of which are inlaid precious stones.

Detail from the entrance of Audience Chamber Inscription in the form a monogram praising Abdülmecid

RECEIVING AMBASSADORS IN THE AUDIENCE CHAMBER

The Audience Chamber, where the sultans were notified of the decisions of the Imperial Council when they had not attended its meetings was, for nearly four centuries, witness to the governing of the Ottoman state. On certain days of the week, members of the council would be received by the sultan following council meetings.

At the start of meetings in the Audience Chamber, the fountains inside and outside the building would be turned on and the sweet splash of the running water would prevent anyone outside from overhearing what was being said within.

Ambassadors would typically be received in the Audience Chamber on the same day that the Janissaries received their pay; in this way, it was hoped, the majesty of the empire would be proven to both friend and foe. The arriving ambassador would first be ushered into the Chamber of the Gatekeeper at the Gate of Salutation where he would receive refreshments in accordance with Ottoman Empire custom. Then, accompanied by the Imperial Council's guardians, he would be led to the Domed Chamber. Though normally three tables were set for the council, five tables would be set on the days when an ambassador was received and the ambassador would dine at the same table as the grand vizier.

If the sultan was so magnanimous as to deign to receive the ambassador, the chief gatekeepers would take the ambassador's arms (both for security reasons and as a show of respect) and lead him into the presence of the sultan. After entering into the sultan's presence, they would salute him from three different points. The sultan was constrained to respect certain rules of protocol: seated in the Throne of State (Serîr-i Saltanat), the sultan would listen to the ambassador through an interpreter, typically a Greek citizen of the empire. Those received into the sultan's presence would not look him in the eye, but rather would remain immobile, holding their hands folded before them, lowering their head, and keeping their eyes cast downward.

In addition to members of the Imperial Council and ambassadors, visiting kings, the khans of the Crimea, and foreign princes would be received in the Audience Chamber as well.

The Library of Sultan Ahmed III

The Library of Sultan Ahmed III

Also known as the Inner Palace Library owing to its location in the courtyard where the palace's inner circle resided, the Library of Sultan Ahmed III is located at the centre of the Inner Palace Courtyard, just behind the Audience Chamber. It is considered a masterpiece of the architecture of the Tulip Period (1718-30). Sultan Ahmed III (r. 1703-30), a calligrapher and bibliophile, had the library built and named after himself in 1718. He had the structure put up in place of the Pool Pavilion, a work of the master architect Sinan that was built on the order of Sultan Selim II (r. 1566-74). In building the library, Ahmed III made it possible for the officials of the Inner Palace to profit from the books found in the palace treasuries.

Though the library is a sign of the importance attributed to scholarship by the people of the court, it is hardly the only such sign. The presence in the palace of two schools (that of the Inner Palace and that of the Harem) also shows that this was

an environment suitable to learning. Nonetheless, the library enabled the many invaluable works in the Inner Treasury, the Privy Room Treasury, and the Harem to be concentrated in a single space and thus better preserved; and this is exactly what is mentioned in the inscription found on the library.

On the library's deed of endowment it is stated that the removal from the palace of any book in the library is prohibited, thus providing precious insight concerning how it was considered a library should be managed. The library's lighting is provided by two rows of 32 windows; this arrangement created a well-lit environment suitable for the reading of books, as well as preventing dampness. The library's doors and window shutters are excellent examples of Ottoman mother-of-pearl and ivory inlay. The tiles in the interior are also elegant examples of the Turkish art of the period. The fountain standing before the library is also a work of the early 18th century.

In 1966 the library's manuscripts were moved to the Mosque of the Aghas of the Inner Palace which is now the Topkapı Palace Library. The library's deed of endowment, the inventory of the works and the shovel with which the library's ground was broken (the same shovel used to break the ground for the Mosque of Sultan Ahmed III) continue to be preserved.

◁ *Ceiling decorations of the Library of Sultan Ahmed III*

The Lesser and The Greater Inner Palace Chambers

As one passes through the Gate of Felicity, the Lesser Inner Palace Chambers are on the left and the Greater Inner Palace Chambers on the right. These chambers served as the palace's educational institutions. Here, were taught the brightest and most attractive children from among those conscripted for state service under the "devşirme" system. Children aged 14 and 15 would study literature, Arabic, Persian, the Islamic sciences (Qur'an recitation, hadith, dogma, fiqh collectively known as Islamic jurisprudence, inheritance law, calligraphy, as well as receiving physical education. Courses in history, geography, geometry, poetry, belles-lettres (inşâ), music, and astronomy were also provided.

In addition to teaching languages, the Inner Palace educational system also provided training in sports such as wrestling and archery as well as military training in the use of weapons such as the sword, the rifle, the cannon, the spear, and played the javelin-based game "jereed". Apart from these, there was also training in the hundreds of ways of wrapping turbans as well as in leatherworking, fletching, the decoration of quivers and the making of saddles. Among the more interesting varieties of education were the training in falconry and hunting with hounds.

In the Inner Palace (where the Ottoman princes were also educated before being sent to govern in the provinces) the education was very strict and its central aim was to discover the children's natural aptitudes. However, the most basic goal of education in the Inner Palace was to train students in how to properly serve and behave at the palace. Students would learn court protocol from Inner Palace officials and etiquette from the Chief of the Gate of Felicity and from the White Eunuchs. Currently, the Lesser and the Greater Inner Palace Chambers (which underwent restoration following a fire in the Inner Palace in 1856) are used as museum service buildings.

The Dormitory Of The Campaigners (Seferli Koğuşu)

The Inner Palace's Campaigner Corps were established in 1635 by Sultan Murad IV. The corps' barracks door has an inscription of restoration bearing the calligraphic seal of Sultan Mehmed V Reşad (r. 1909-18) and was originally constructed at the beginning of the 18th century on the order of Sultan Ahmed III.

The duty of the corps was to launder the sultan's turbans and personal clothing and to accompany him on campaigns. The prayer mat on which the sultan would pray in the mosque would be laid out by the Chief of the Campaigners. The Campaigner Corps were initially charged with the duty of laundering the clothes of the people resident in the Inner Palace, as well as with the general upkeep of the Inner Palace but later came to embrace more professional and

artistic activities such as archery, wrestling, singing, and hairdressing.

The Dormitory of the Campaigners, a structure with two separate spaces, is currently used as an exhibition space for the clothing of the sultans.

The Pavilion of The Conqueror / The Treasury Pavilion / The Inner Palace Treasury

The Pavilion of the Conqueror was built in 1462-63 and is located on a point with a commanding and beautiful view of the whole of Sarayburnu. With great mastery, it was constructed on a highly inconvenient slope and follows the plan of Turkish houses containing an external hall. The pavilion is made up of four main rooms and has a central roofed hall with an ablution fountain and a semi-open portico. The overseer of the Treasury Dormitory and of the Inner Palace Treasury was called the "hazîne kethüdası".

Plunder obtained after the Battle of Chaldiran on 23 August 1514 and the conquest of Mamluk Egypt in 1517 enabled Sultan Selim I or "Selim the Grim" (r. 1512-20) (the grandson of Sultan Mehmed II) to greatly enrich the palace treasury. Having thus filled the treasury, Selim commanded: "Let this treasury which I have filled with gold bear the seal of whichever of my successors can thus fill it with loot; otherwise, let it continue to bear my own seal." And indeed, the external door of the Inner Palace Treasury continued to bear Selim's seal until the palace was finally converted into a museum.

Use of the Royal Treasury (Hazîne-i Hümâyûn) was subject to the sultan's discretion. The treasury's gold and silver would be used for administration of the palace, for public works, construction and for philanthropic purposes.

Taxes from Egypt effectively constituted the sultan's private "pocket money" (Ceb-i Hümâyûn) and would be used to cover the expenses of buildings constructed on his order such as mosques, fountains, and madrasas or schools of theology, some of which have survived to the present. When state finances were strained, such as in times of war, the sultan would dip into the Royal Treasury so as to lend to the state treasury but would never subsequently ask for repayment. The other section of the treasury was an exhibition hall of sorts. Here were exhibited the sultan's share of plunder, gifts from ambassadors, and precious objects of historical value that had been purchased. Among these objects were gold and silver pots and pans; silk carpets and prayer mats; precious furs; gem-studded clothes and kaftans; feather plumes; armbands; riding equipment; belts; and diamonds, pearls, turquoise, rubies and emeralds.

In the 19th century, these precious objects were exhibited to foreign dignitaries in specially constructed showcases; this is now considered to be the first museum-style activity to have been carried out in Turkey. The objects that make up the Royal Treasury continue to be exhibited at the Pavilion of the Conqueror.

The Butlers' Dormitory (Kilerli Koğuşu)

The Butlers' Dormitory was a section of the palace charged both with maintaining the palace's storerooms (kiler) and with serving the sultan. Those who worked here were respected palace employees who were quite close to him. The most important duties of the butlers were to cook the sultan's food, lay the tables, wait on the tables (and clear them after meals), keep the silverware, and wash the dishes. Additionally, they were responsible for providing food and beverages to and maintaining the Harem's storeroom. They would also provide and light the candles in the large candelabrums found in the rooms of the palace, in the palace mosques, and in the room where the holy relics were kept. Another duty of the butlers was to collect the waters of April showers and present them to the sultan, who would then pay them a gratuity for this service.

For the butlers to carry out all of these services, they were required to be in a state of ritual cleanliness (âbdest). All of the duties accorded to the Butlers' Dormitory were, in fact, required to be done according to a certain method. The Chief Butler (kilercibaşı), who had in his service several hundred employees, was also charged with the supervision of the employees working in the Imperial Kitchens in the Outer Palace (Bîrûn). The Butlers' Dormitory burned down in 1856 and was subsequently rebuilt. Currently, the building houses the Topkapı Palace Museum Offices.

The Dormitory Of The Treasury (Hazîne Koğuşu)

Responsibility for the Inner Palace Treasury (Enderûn Hazînesi) and for the palace's jewellery and other precious items fell to those resident in this building which came to be known as the Dormitory of the Treasury or the Dormitory of the Treasury Guards (Hazîne Koğuşu). This building was constructed in the time of Sultan Mehmed II (r. 1451-81) and maintained its importance in the palace throughout the centuries. It burned down in the fire of 1856 and was subsequently rebuilt by Sultan Abdülmecid. The building is currently used as an exhibition hall.

The Treasury Of The Chamberlain (Silâhdâr Hazînesi)

The Treasury of the Chamberlain is adjacent to the building where the holy relics are housed. Here were stored the precious objects entrusted to the chamberlain: the sultan's weapons, such as swords, maces, shields, and armor; the golden candelabra of the Privy Room and the Pavilion Hall; a certain amount of money that was used as "pocket money" by the sultan and was not kept in the treasury proper; those holy relics that were not kept in the Privy Room; the old draperies used at the Kaaba and environs (Harem-i Şerîf) in Mecca, which would be sent back to Istanbul when the new draperies had been sent; old Qur'ans; and highly valuable old manuscripts.

Currently, the Treasury of the Chamberlain is used for temporary exhibitions of the holy relics.

The Privy Room (Has Oda) / The Chamber Of The Holy Relics (Mukaddes Emanetler Dairesi)

The Privy Room, built during the time of Sultan Mehmed II (r. 1451-81) as the sultan's private apartments on the courtyard of the Inner Palace, is a two-storey structure of four basic spaces. The first part, at the entrance, is the Fountain Hall, named for the fountain located beneath the first dome. Beneath the second dome is a bench on which the sultan could sit. The wooden doors and window shutters open onto the Petition Room and the other rooms and date back to the building's initial construction. Above them is inscribed the name of Mehmed II. The mother-of-pearl inlay door in the Privy Room was installed during renovations in 1916.

The Petition Room (Arzhâne) is entered through a door on the right side of the Fountain Hall and on this door is written verse 46 of the Qur'an's Surah al-Hijr: "Enter in peace and security!" (udkhuluha bisalamin aminina). In here, the sultan would read petitions submitted to him and issue appropriate orders related to them. It was also the room where he would receive guests. The Petition Room is decorated with Iznik and Kütahya tiles manufactured at the

The marble fireplace in the Privy Room

workshops established in the Palace of the Porphyrogenitus (Tekfur Sarayı) now located in modern-day Istanbul's Fatih district. Containing tiles from several different periods and in several different styles, the Petition Room is effectively a fine ceramic tile exhibition in itself. In the band stretching among the tiles are inscribed verses 38 to 44 of the Qur'an's Surah al-Ahzab; the sections following the final verse are located precisely in the centre of the Privy Room's dome.

One additional use of the Petition Room was as a place for the sultan to receive the congratulations of the grand vizier and other court dignitaries following his accession to the throne as well as during official visits to the Holy Mantle of the Prophet which took place on the fifteenth day of the month of Ramadan. Currently, the Petition Room is open to the public and some of the holy relics are exhibited here.

The Privy Room was primarily a place used in the winter as a study. In particular, the sultans Mehmed II, Bayezid II, Selim I, and Suleiman the Magnificent would spend a large part of their days here, and would on occasion spend the night here when there was a great deal of state business. The Privy Room's dome was raised on the order of Sultan Selim I following his conquest of Mamluk Egypt and uses Mamluk-style honeycomb corbels. This dome is much higher than the other domes-

The Fountain Hall, located at the entrance to the Privy Room/Chamber of the Holy Relics

The Pavillion of the Holy Mantle

another sign indicating the fact that this was a room used by the sultan.

In the left corner of the Privy Room stands a gilded throne made of silver covered by a canopy. This throne was made in the time of Sultan Murad IV (r. 1623-40) by the court's chief jeweler, Dervish Zıllî Mehmed who is also known as the father of famed author and traveler Evliyâ Çelebi. The throne's canopy is done as a cavetto vault and rests on four columns. Beautiful carvings and a hadith inscription decorate it, along with a panegyric written about this particular throne by the poet Cevrî. When a prince was to be enthroned, he would first sit here before proceeding to the enthronement ceremony at the Gate of Felicity. It was also here that the grand vizier and the shaykhu'l-Islam would swear their loyalty to the sultan. Before the official ceremony, two cycles of Islamic prayer (raka`ah) would be recited here. Until the time of Mahmud II (r. 1808-39), the two faces of the throne were covered with silver grilles and the holy relics were stored here together with the drawer holding the Holy Mantle of the Prophet.

Though the Privy Room is not in fact particularly large, its ceramic tile panels and imposing

The Gate of the Privy Room

dome make it appear larger than it is. Inscribed in white sülüs calligraphy over a dark blue base on the tile panels is the Arab poet al-Busiri's poem Nahja'l-Burdah ("The True Path of the Mantle") in praise of the Prophet Muhammad. Due to the poem's presence here in the room where the Holy Mantle of the Prophet was kept, this poem is also known as "The Panegyric of the Mantle" (Hırka Kasîdesi) in Turkish. The Holy Mantle of the Prophet, or the Mantle of Felicity (Hırka-i Saâdet), has been kept in the Privy Room ever since it was brought from Egypt following Selim I's conquest in 1517. When the Ottoman

sultans formally took on the Islamic caliphate, various holy relics continued to be brought here following the reign of Selim as well. When Topkapı Palace was abandoned in the 19th century, the Privy Room began to be used solely to house and preserve the holy relics and, over time, the entire structure became known as the Chamber of the Holy Relics (Mukaddes Emanetler Dairesi).

The Privy Room is currently closed to the public.

The Sundial

The sundial in front of the Privy Room was

constructed during the reign of Sultan Mehmed II for the purpose of indicating times of prayer. The inscription on it states that it was repaired in the time of Sultan Mustafa III (r. 1757-74).

The Incense Mortar

The marble mortar located on the side of the Privy Room that faces the courtyard was used in Ottoman times to catch the dust generated by the cleaning of the Holy Mantle of the Prophet, thus saving it from being trampled on. The inscription contains a Persian expression concerning the mortar.

The Privy Room Aghas

The Privy Room Aghas came from the highest ranks of the Inner Palace school. The young boys (iç oğlanları) who were to be primed for this group were chosen from among the school's best and brightest pupils. The Privy Room Aghas would spend all their time in the presence or proximity of the sultan, and were charged not only with serving him, but also with the maintenance and preservation of the holy relics. When the dormitory of the Privy Room Aghas was converted into the Handcloth Room in the 19th century, the colonnaded inner courtyard in front of the building was enclosed and turned into a dormitory. Currently, this space is used to exhibit the portraits of the sultans.

The Mosque of The Aghas of The Inner Palace (Enderûn Ağalar Câmii)

Located adjacent to the Privy Room, the Mosque of the Aghas of the Inner

The Mosque Of The Aghas Of The Inner Palace

Palace was built in the time of Sultan Mehmed II for use by the sultan, the white eunuchs, and the pupils of the Inner Palace school. As the palace's oldest, largest, and most central mosque, it was placed diagonally to the courtyard because it had to face in the direction of the Kaaba in Mecca. Its interior is decorated with early 17th-century Iznik tiles as well as 18th-century tiles produced in the workshops established at the Palace of the Porphyrogenitus (Tekfur Sarayı).

Currently, the Mosque of the Aghas of the Inner Palace is used as the Topkapı Palace Library. Among the many invaluable manuscripts found here are not only works in Ottoman Turkish, Arabic, and Persian, but also manuscripts written in Greek and in Slavic languages.

The Aviary and The Harem Gate

In the corner of the Inner Palace Courtyard just beside the Lesser Inner Palace Chamber, there once stood a small inner courtyard called the Aviary Courtyard. From there, one could enter the Harem using the gate known as the Aviary Gate. In the inscription above this gate, it is related that the Aviary kitchens were restored in 1734-35 by Sultan Mahmud I. Currently, this gate is used as the exit gate of the Harem. The Aviary itself stands before the gate, and has two chambers, one on top of the other in the style of traditional aviaries.

THE HAREM

At Topkapı Palace, the Harem Apartments were where the sultans lived together with their families. Reflecting architectural styles ranging from the 16th century to the early 19th century, the entire complex is of the greatest importance in terms of architectural history. The Harem was initially established within the Second Courtyard above the palace's back gardens and expanded greatly over the centuries. The apartments were secluded with great care by means of high walls, from the more public courtyards and sections of the palace where government business was conducted.

Soon after Topkapı Palace was constructed, the Old Palace (located in the Bayezid neighborhood of Istanbul) began to be used solely as the harem, while Topkapı Palace became the seat of government and of public functions (which together were called "selamlık"). However, there are also some sources stating that, during this same period, a small harem, the Girls' Palace (Sarây-ı Duhterân), was also built beside the palace's Golden Road. The Harem developed in four stages, with perhaps the most intense period of construction and organization occurring when Sultan Suleiman the Magnificent (r. 1520-66) moved into the Topkapı Palace harem together with his Haseki ("favorite") Hürrem Sultan (known as Roxelana in the West)

△ *An engraving of the Harem as imagined by Antoine-Ignace Melling*

▷ *Entrance of the Harem*

and his family; this period continued until the 18th century.

The Harem contains more than 300 rooms, nine bathhouses, two mosques, a hospital, dormitories, and a laundry. The basic plan of the Harem consists of consecutive courtyards surrounded by and interspersed with living quarters, rooms, pavilions, and service buildings.

The Domed Cabinets, The Fountain Hall And The Mosque Of The Eunuchs

An inscription found above the Gate of Carriages and dated 1587 states that the gate was constructed in that year on the orders of Sultan Murad III as the entrance to the Harem Apartments. Beyond this gate are the Domed Cabinets, with the cabinets being found in the walls of this room. Here, the documents concerning the pious foundation connected to the holy sites in Mecca and Medina were kept. This foundation was under the supervision of the Chief Black Eunuch (Dârüssaâde Ağası). The Fountain Hall, which was managed by the black eunuchs, was the main entrance to the Harem. It was through this area, with its walls covered in 17th-century Kütahya ceramic tiles, that the sultans would pass when they went to observe a military procession or (having disguised themselves) when they wished to go outside. The small mosque found on the left after leaving the Fountain Hall was rebuilt following the fire of 1665. Its walls, too, are decorated with 17th-century tiles, these ones bearing floral motifs and verses of the Qur'an.

The Fountain Hall

The Courtyard of the Black Eunuchs

The Paved Courtyard Of The Black Eunuchs

The Paved Courtyard of the Black Eunuchs was named after the Black Eunuchs. Their main duty was to guard the Harem entrance, checking whoever went in and out and making sure that no one unwanted was allowed in. It is surrounded by the Treasurer's Chamber; the Chamber of the Courtiers; the Dormitory of the Black Eunuchs and the School of the Princes, which had an educational function like that of the dormitories found in the Inner Palace Courtyard the Schools of the Princes. It is known that the sultan would ride on horseback along the road, paved with podima stones.

The Harem Eunuchs And The Black Eunuchs

Assigning the task of guarding the women's section of a royal palace to eunuchs is a very ancient Mesopotamian tradition going back to the Assyrians and was subsequently adopted in palaces as distant as China and Rome. This tradition was also practiced in the Harem of the Ottoman sultans. By the end of the 16th century, the duty of guarding the concubines had fallen exclusively to the Black Eunuchs who held this power until the very end of the empire, increasing their power all the while. Black children from Central Africa, and from Abyssinia in particular, would be chosen for this position, and then, having been introduced into the harems of the Old Palace

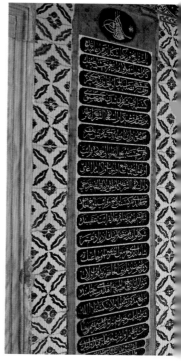

and Topkapı Palace, would be educated according to a strict regimen.

The Main Gate (Cümle Kapısı)

The Harem's Main Gate (also known as the Royal Gate (Saltanat Kapısı)) opens onto the guardhouse, to which are connected the Harem's three main divisions. This area is a domed vestibule with arches. The door on the left leads through the Gallery of the Concubines to the Paved Courtyard of the Concubines and Wives. The door in the center leads to the Paved Courtyard of the Queen Mother (known as the Vâlide Sultan) and the door on the right leads to the Golden Road and the sultan's private apartments.

Windows of the Dormitory of the Black Eunuchs

Gate separating the Harem from the Paved Courtyard of the Black Eunuchs

The Paved Courtyard of The Wives and The Paved Courtyard of The Concubines

The Harem of Topkapı Palace (which was supported by many other dynastic palaces, particularly the Old Palace) made up one branch of the Ottoman devşirme system of recruiting young children and training them for state service.

The courtyard, the smallest in the Harem and which opens onto the Wives' Apartments and the Concubines' Dormitories is known due to its location as both the Paved Courtyard of the Wives and the Paved Courtyard of the Concubines.

The long and narrow courtyard is connected on one side to the area of the Black Eunuchs and on the other to the Paved Courtyard of the Queen Mother and the Chamber of the Master Craftsmen. After passing through this courtyard, one arrives at the section where the women of the Harem lived.

It is believed that the Apartments of the Wives and the Apartment of the Queen Mother located on this courtyard were built in the time of Sultan Murad III (r. 1574-95). There were three separate apartments for the wives. Each one having two storeys, fireplaces and tiled walls.

The Paved Courtyard of the Wives and Concubines

Concubine adorning herself

CONCUBINES

Most of the concubines in the Harem were Circassians from the Caucasus although there were Arab and black concubines as well. All were taken into the palace between the ages of 5 and 16. Their education was similar to that received by the boys of the Inner Palace: they would first be taught Turkish and the etiquette of the palace. The majority of concubines would be taken for employment as servants and they would, after an initial period of training, be transferred to services related to the laundry, the bathhouse furnaces, the pantries, and meal service. Those deemed pretty and intelligent, however, would be trained by experienced women according to their particular aptitudes, learning such things as reading and writing, sewing, embroidery, music, and dancing. The highest-ranking women of the palace bore the title Kadın, literally meaning "woman" or "lady".

Those concubines who became "favorites" (known as has odalık, gözde, or ikbâl) or who bore the sultan a child would be raised to the status of wife (Kadın Efendi) or favorite wife (Haseki Sultan). Not all of the concubines chosen and educated for the sultan would be taken into the Harem; some of these girls would be given in marriage to men of appropriate importance and would live outside of the palace.

Miniature depicting female musicians in the Harem in the 18th century by Levni

Birth scene in the Harem

The Apartments Of The Wives

The Apartments of the Wives were the residences of those who had born the sultan a child. These apartments, whose lower levels were used as dormitories for servant concubines, are generally believed to have been built at the same time as the Apartment of the Queen Mother (approximately 1585; during the reign of Sultan Murad III). It is also thought that it was the sultan's wives (or "Kadın Efendi") who lived in these apartments, and that they were closer to the sultan's mother than they were to the sultan himself.

The Harem Hospital

On the paved courtyard of the hospital, also known as the Courtyard of the Concubines, were the two-storey stone dormitory of the concubines. The floorsa were laid with carpets from Şirvan in the southeast of modern-day Turkey. There was a bathhouse (hamam); a laundry; a sick ward; a kitchen for hospital

Courtyard of the Queen Mother

patients; a chamber for the final ablution of the dead; and the Gate of the Dead (Meyyit Kapısı), where the funerals of concubines were begun. This section of the Harem is reached by means of the stone stairs known as the "40 Steps".

The Apartment Of The Queen Mother (Vâlide Sultan Dairesi)

The Paved Courtyard of the Queen Mother (the Vâlide Sultan) was for centuries at the center of the life of the Ottoman dynasty and of the Harem, particularly the women of the Harem's upper class. It is believed that the buildings extending along the Golden Road side of this courtyard were constructed in the 15th century and the first half of the 16th century. When the Apartment of the Queen Mother and the bathhouse were constructed in the 16th century, this area became an enclosed inner courtyard.

The Apartment of the Queen Mother

The Apartment of the Queen Mother, reminiscent of the sultan's own apartment with its well-ordered and detailed arrangement, was constructed by Sultan Murad III (r. 1574-95) for his mother Nurbanu Sultan. A second floor was added in the late 18th century by Sultan Selim III (r. 1789-1807) for use by his mother, Mihrişah Sultan, and himself. The apartment has a strong rococo décor and is hung with numerous landscape paintings. The apartment has tiled walls at floor level, fireplaces and fountains in each of the rooms, and numerous floral decorations. On the apartment's lower floor is a hall, a bedroom, and a prayer room, where the Queen Mother would spend much of her day. After meals, the Queen Mother would enjoy herself

by watching dancers and singers from among the concubines', or by listening to a recital from the Qur'an done by an experienced reciter or a reading from a history book. Sources also inform us that favorites of the sultan would visit the Queen Mother here. With its bathhouse, toilet, and living quarters, the Apartment of the Queen Mother effectively constituted an independently functioning structure.

The Bathhouse (Hamam) of The Sovereign and The Bathhouse of The Queen Mother

This structure was built in the late 16th century as a double bathhouse (hamam), and underwent renovations in the mid-18th century. Both bathhouses are built to a similar plan, with cold, warm, and hot sections. The Bathhouse of the Queen Mother, however, is smaller than the Bathhouse

The trussed section where the sultans used to wash in the Bathhouse of the Sovereign

of the Sovereign. These bathhouses also served to separate the sultan's apartments from the part of the Harem where the women lived. According to the day, the Bathhouse of the Queen Mother would be used by different classes of women: wives, servants, or concubines.

The faucet of the Sultan's Hamam

The Hamam of the Sovereign as depicted by Mouradgea d'Obsson

The Imperial Hall

The Hall of the Sovereign / The Throne Hall

The Hall of the Sovereign, located between the Privy Room of Sultan Murad III and the bathhouses, is the second largest domed space in the Harem. From written sources and panoramic paintings of Topkapı Palace, it is apparent that it was constructed sometime in the 1580s, after the Privy Room of Sultan Murad III.

The structure's current state reflects the various repairs and alterations undergone over the course of centuries. The ceramics stretching the length of the walls and decorated with various inscriptions were placed here following the fire of 1665 with the blue-white Dutch ceramics being set in the mid-18th century.

The Privy Room of Sultan Murad III

The Privy Room Of Sultan Murad III

The Privy Room of Sultan Murad III is as important in terms of Ottoman architecture as the Harem itself. It was designed and built by the chief architect Sinan in 1579 on the order of the sultan and used as the sultans' official and private apartment. Its walls are covered with 16th-century İznik tiles. One of the walls has been inscribed, in white writing over blue, with the Verse of the Throne from the Qur'an's Surah al-Baqarah (2:255). On the lower level of the room is a bay window constructed by Sultan Ahmed I (r. 1603-17) and a pool dated 1579.

The Privy Room of Sultan Ahmed I

This room was built in 1608 at the request of Sultan Ahmed I. Its walls are covered with predominantly green tiles while its windows and cabinet doors are decorated with classical mother-of-pearl inlay.

The Privy Room of Sultan Ahmed III / The Fruit Room

This small room of Sultan Ahmed III (r.1703-30) is located between the Hall of the Sovereign and the Privy Room of Sultan Ahmed I, both of which have entrances into the room.

This room was constructed during the Tulip Period of 1718-30, named for the period's great interest in and demand for flowers and in particular tulips. The reign of Sultan Ahmed III is recognized as the most glorious period of a new style in the Ottoman decorative arts, a style influenced primarily by the Tulip Period. This new style, which can be considered naturalistic, was reflected in all of the architectural works of the period, whether in painting and calligraphy or in work done in plaster and marble relief. The Privy Room of Sultan Ahmed III is also known as the Fruit Room (Yemiş Odası) owing to the paintings of fruit platters and vases of flowers that completely cover its walls and immerse visitors in a veritable springtime atmosphere.

The Privy Room of Sultan Ahmed III / The Fruit Room

The Privy Room of Sultan Ahmed I

The Twin Pavilions and The Apartment of The Crown Prince

The Twin Pavilions were constructed in stages in the 17th century on the side of the Central Courtyard next to the entrance of the Privy Room of Sultan Murad III. Beginning in the 18th century, these rooms were used as the Apartment of the Crown Prince. The walls are embellished with 17th-century İznik tiles while the golden decorations on the wooden dome are quite original.

Interior of the Twin Kioks

Interior of the Twin Kioks

△ *The Twin Kiosks*

▽ *The Apartment of the Favorites and the Chamberlain's Courtyard*

The Apartment of The Favorites and The Chamberlain's Courtyard

Unlike the other courtyards, the Chamberlain's Courtyard is not entirely enclosed but rather remains open on one side. With the open side looking onto the Harem's pool, the side of the courtyard that looks onto the Paved Courtyard of the Queen Mother contains the portico known as the Council Place of the Djinn. The upper floor of this portico is the Princes' Apartments.

When the Apartment of the Favorites was built within the Chamberlain's Courtyard in the mid-18th century, the living quarters of the women were connected, for the first time, to the living quarters of the sultan. The apartment's rows of rooms have extensions that jut outward, facing the terrace and allowing access between the different rooms. It is a widespread view that the first-floor apartment of Sultan Abdülhamid I (r. 1774-89) was previously known as the Tower of Selim I (r. 1512-20). While this secluded tower and its bathhouse had formerly been used by the princes, following the construction of the Apartment of the

Favorites it became the residence of Abdülhamid I and his family. Within this structure are also found a treasury constructed of stone with doors of bronze and a room of mirrors.

The Golden Road (Altın Yol)

The Golden Road is the Harem's longest, oldest, and most important passageway. It is a vaulted road running the length of the wall that separates the Harem from the Inner Palace Courtyard. The most noteworthy feature of the Golden Road is the colonnaded section in the Harem that passes through the Hall of the Sovereign, defining the edges of the Central Courtyard and the Harem Garden.

Before it became known as the Golden Road in the 19th century, this passageway was variously known as the Long Road (Uzun Yol), the Sultan's Path (Rah-ı Pâdişâhî), and the Avenue of His Excellency the Sultan (Sokak-ı Hazret-i Pâdişâhî), and was generally used by the sultan as a shortcut to the Harem apartments. The name "Golden Road" does not come from the road's appearance (which is quite unadorned with its plastered walls and stone pavement) but rather from the fact that when the sultan would pass through here on certain special days, he would throw gold coins to the Harem's inhabitants who would be standing all along the road.

Wall tile panels

Tile panels from the Golden Road

The Double Colonnade of the Privy Chamber

THE FOURTH COURTYARD
THE ROYAL HALL

The terrace known as the Royal Hall or the Marble Hall is the highest spot in the Fourth Courtyard and is the area onto which the double-columned portico of the Privy Room opens. This space, made up of a flower garden and a marble terrace with a pool, is one of the favorite sites in Topkapı Palace. The pool, located in front of the portico, contains a jet of water and was once larger but construction in the 17th century by Sultan Murad IV (r. 1623-40) and Sultan İbrahim I (r. 1640-48) resulted in the pool's being narrowed and the widening of the terrace in the direction of the Golden Horn. In the Fourth Courtyard are found the Circumcision Chamber, the Iftar Gazebo, the Yerevan Pavilion and the Baghdad Pavilion.

Sultan Ahmed III throwing gold to servants in the Royal Hall (the Marble Hall), with princes resting in Baghdad Pavilion following circumcision (from the Sûrnâme-i Vehbi, 1720)

From this courtyard, located which is also a garden with tulips and other flowers, one descends a three-meter long staircase to the Royal Hall where the Pavilion Hall and the Tower of the Chief Physician are. The lowest terrace in this direction, which is toward the Marmara Sea, contains the Mecidiye Pavilion, the Garment Room and the Mosque of the Hall.

The Circumcision Chamber

The Circumcision Chamber is a rectangular room with a small adjunct at the back, and was built in the time of Sultan Suleiman the Magnificent (r. 1520-66). It later underwent various restorations, acquiring its current appearance in the time of Sultan İbrahim II (r.1640-48).

The name "Circumcision Chamber" was not given until later when the space was used for the circumcision of the sons of Sultan Ahmed III (r. 1703-30). It is also said to have been the room where the sultan slept in the summertime.

Tiles of the Circumcision Chamber

Tile panels of the Circumcision Chamber

Though the Circumcision Chamber is hardly outstanding from an architectural point of view, it is unique owing to the 16th- and 17th-century tiles on its inner and outer surfaces. There are tombac-grated fireplace, marble window basins, and inscribed fountains but in particular, what stands out are the monolithic blue-white ceramics with "Chi-lin" figures, found on the chamber's outer surface and done in the "saz" style.

FLORAL TASTES OF THE OTTOMAN PALACE

Flowers were always accorded great importance in the Ottoman palace. After Sultan Mehmed II (r. 1451-81) constructed Topkapı Palace. He set aside large tracts of land-both within the palace grounds and throughout Istanbul-for the growing of flowers, assigning 920 gardeners to their care. Sultan Suleiman the Magnificent (r. 1520-66) was a sultan known not only for his interest in flowers, but also for his own gardening skills; this interest is reflected in the tulip-bedecked tiles, miniatures, embroidery, fabrics, carpets, fountains, buildings and tombstones constructed in his time. In the palace gardens, the favoured flowers (apart from the ubiquitous tulip) were roses, hyacinths, orange tulips or "flava", irises, and carnations.

Nonetheless, few flowers were as exalted by the Ottoman court, particularly in the 16th and 17th centuries, as the tulip, which even lent its name to a period of history: the Tulip Period of 1718-30. The long, thin, and etiolated variety known as the "Istanbul tulip" became highly valuable and was sold for extremely high prices reminiscent of those found during the 1630s "tulipomania" of Holland. The tulip was not present in the gardens of the Byzantine Empire but was apparently known by the Seljuks, judging from its frequent appearance as a motif in tiles of the Seljuk era. It was was hence first introduced to Europe during the reign of Suleiman the Magnificent by Ogier Ghiselin de Busbecq, the Austrian ambassador to the Ottoman court. The word "tulip" is derived from tülbent, the Turkish word for the fine muslin used to make turbans. Pierre Belon, a French botanist of the same period, had observed tulips inserted into turbans and the word for the flower was either mistaken by de Busbecq for the word for the turban, or else the flower was likened by Europeans to that particular piece of headgear.

However, the tulip was by no means the only flower variety de Busbecq introduced to Europe: he was also responsible for the introduction of the saffron crocus, the jonquil, the lilac, the hyacinth, the narcissus, and the horse chestnut (none of which were known in northern Europe at the time).

The Yerevan Pavilion

This pavilion was constructed in 1636 to commemorate Sultan Murad IV's victory at the city of Yerevan in modern-day Armenia. The pavilion's architect is believed to have been Koca Kasım Ağa, the Chief Architect of the time. Within the octagonal pavilion is a copper fireplace plated with gold while the pavilion's vaulted dome and hall are richly decorated with hand-drawn patterns in gold leaf. The window shutters and cabinet doors are wooden with mother-of-pearl inlay. The outer façade of the pavilion features Mamluk-style marble panels reaching up to the upper windows while the part above the windows is decorated in patterned ceramic tiles.

The Yerevan Pavilion was used to store the sultan's ceremonial turbans as well as being the space where the Holy Relics were cleaned in the month of Ramadan. The pavilion also once held handwritten manuscripts which were kept in the library established here when Sultan Mahmud I (r. 1730-54) put together a collection of precious books for the dignitaries of the Privy Room. This library was later expanded by Sultans Osman III (r. 1754-57) and Mustafa III (r. 1757-74). The manuscripts are currently kept in the Topkapı Palace Museum Library.

The Baghdad Pavilion

The construction of the Baghdad Pavilion began just as Sultan Murad IV embarked on his Baghdad Campaign in April 1638. By the time the sultan returned in June of the following years, the pavilion's decorations remained unfinished and the building could only be completed after the sultan's death on 8th February 1640.

This structure is the most unique and beautiful example of pavilion architecture. Raised atop the octagonal foundations is a vaulted cellar with stone arches resting on pillars seven meters in height. In three of the pavilion's recesses there are doors while in the fourth there is a fireplace. The lower and upper floors both have four windows each.

The pavilion has a rather classical décor with cushioned divan seats along the walls, in which there are niches covered with green and blue 15th-century İznik tiles. The floral patterns found on the dome are done on gazelle leather,

the style of the time. The window shutters and cabinet doors are of ebony with mother-of-pearl, turtle shell, and ivory inlay.

The classical fireplace is one of the Baghdad Pavilion's most unique elements. The fireplace's interior is plated with lead; a precaution against fire. The two sides of the fireplace are decorated in exquisite ceramic tiles featuring bird figures. Two other important works found in the Baghdad Pavilion are the hanging ball inside a tombac grille and the silver brazier which was a gift of French king Louis XIV, both of which are traditional symbols of sovereignty.

The Baghdad Pavilion, originally built to commemorate the reconquest of Baghdad by Sultan Murad IV in the mid-17th century, is Topkapı Palace's best preserved building. It was also here that the Cabinet of Ministers (Meclis-i Vükelâ) met during the last years of the Ottoman Empire.

The Iftar Pergola

Constructed in 1640 during the reign of Sultan İbrahim, this small pergola juts out from the courtyard between the Baghdad Pavilion and the Circumcision Chamber. The structure has a roof that features a tulip-shaped device and is supported by four gold-plated copper columns. In addition to its use for holiday festivities, the pergola was also the place where sultans would break their fast in the evening (known as iftar) whenever the month of Ramadan fell in the summertime.

The Sofa Pavilion (Kara Mustafa Pasha Pavilion)

Though the exact date of the initial construction of this pavilion is unknown, it is sometimes called the Sofa Pavilion due to the fact that it was built sometime during the 1676-83 grand viziership of Kara Mustafa Pasha. Two inscriptions on the building reveal that it underwent restoration during the reigns of Sultan Ahmed III (r. 1703-30) and Sultan Mahmud I (r. 1730-54).

The most important work in Sofa Pavilion's inventory is a gold-plated bronze brazier signed "Duplesis". It was sent to

The Sofa Pavillion

Sultan Mahmud I by the French King Louis XV in 1742. The building also features Louis XV tables, candelabra, and cabinets. This pavilion was the first example of a new style that has since come be to be called "Turkish Rococo" and it had a great influence on 18th-century residential architecture; particularly on the seaside mansions, found along the Bosphorus.

Tower Of The Chief Physician / Tower Of The Chief Tutor

The Tower of the Chief Tutor, built atop the walls encircling the palace, was constructed in the time of Sultan Mehmed II (r. 1451-81). This two-storey tower acquired its current appearance following alterations made in the time of Sultan Abdülmecid (r. 1839-61). Each of its four sides contains a window, and there is an iron door on the tower's front side.

Tower of the Chief Physician

Inside the tower and just to the right of the entrance is a door behind which a 14-step staircase leads to the tower's upper floor.

The structure is called the Chamber of the Chief Physician owing to the fact that it was the place of employment of the physician who served the sultan and his family. It was also known also as the Tower of the Chief Tutor, since, within the hierarchy of the court, the Chief Physician served under the Chief Tutor. One of the main duties of the Chief Physician was to observe the pharmacist as he prepared the medicines the former had prescribed for the sultan. Once the medicines had been placed in a bottle, bowl, or other container, the Chief Physician would then seal them and present them to the sultan. The tower's lower floor, restored in 1982, has been set up as a space for the exhibition of pharmaceutical instruments and materials.

The Mecidiye Pavilion and The Garment Room

The Mecidiye Pavilion, also called the Mecidiye Imperial Pavilion (Mecîdiye Kasr-ı Hümâyûnu), received its name because it was built for Sultan Abdülmecid. Constructed in 1858 by the architect Serkis Balyan, it was the last pavilion built in the palace and so also goes by the name "New Pavilion". Like the Garment Room, constructed at the same time, the building shows the influence of 19th-century European art.

On the open side of the pavilion, there is a large marble terrace with a view. The pavilion stands atop a supporting wall dating back to Byzantine times. Formerly, the space on which it stands was occupied by the Tent Pavilion and another pavilion, built in the time of Sultan Mehmed II (r. 1451-81).

This later kiosk was used by sultans when they came to the palace on the occasion of visits

to the Holy Relics, of enthronement ceremonies, or of other religious or official ceremonies. The kiosk was made up of two sections, the Reception Section with its large hall and two reception rooms, and the Harem Section. The interior of the Reception Section was decorated with French furniture since foreign dignitaries would be received here. The console, wardrobes, mirrors and piano decorated with the Boule technique are particularly noteworthy.

The Mosque Of The Hall / The Sofa Mosque

It is thought that the Mosque of the Hall was constructed in the time of Sultan Mahmud II (r. 1808-39) following the demolition of the Chamberlain's Pavilion.

The inscription on the door of the mosque states that it underwent restoration in 1858, during the reign of Sultan Abdülmecid. Currently, the mosque is open for any visitors who might like to perform their regular prayers here.

CHINESE AND JAPANESE PORCELAINS

Among the most invaluable collections in the Topkapı Palace Museum is its Chinese porcelain collection, displayed in the palace's Imperial Kitchens (Matbah-ı Âmire) together with the Japanese porcelain collection. This unique collection, which consists of more than 10,000 pieces, is the largest porcelain collection outside of China and is particularly important in that it showcases the uninterrupted historical development of porcelain from the 13th century to the early 20th century. The collection is made up of porcelains manufactured in China for the Islamic markets of the Middle and Near East and in this way resembles the Ardabil collection at the Archaeological Museum of Iran in Tehran.

The palace collection is made up primarily of porcelains and celadon ware produced in the kilns of Longquan and Jingdezhen in China during the Yuan (1271-1368), Ming (1368-1644) and Qing (1644-1912) dynasties. The largest part of the collection consists of richly decorated large bowls and plates suitable for the food cultures and eating habits found in Muslim countries.

The current palace collection has been assembled largely by means of war plunder, gifts, and unclaimed inheritances; there are also several purchased works. Although no archival documents concerning orders or direct purchases from China have been found, it is clear from price and auction records from the second half of the 16th century onwards, that Chinese porcelains began to be purchased by court dignitaries and the wealthy.

The pieces in the palace's Chinese porcelain collection can be classified into four basic types: celadon ware, blue-whites, monochromes and polychromes.

Celadon Ware

The celadon ware collection of Topkapı Palace is the world's largest, consisting of 1,354 pieces of which nearly all were made during the 14th and 15th centuries under the Yuan and Ming dynasties. Ottomans, like those in other Islamic countries, preferred celadon tableware because it was believed to reveal the presence of poison. Celadon tableware continued to be used in Ottoman mansions in the 19th century, and was sometimes included in dowries.

Celadon green glazed bottle, Qing Dynasty. Late 17th- Early 18th centuries

Celadon ewer, early Ming Dynasty, China

Blue-Whites

The Topkapı Palace collection includes 5,373 pieces of blue and white porcelain dating from the middle of the 14th century to the 19th century. Nearly all of these were produced in the kilns of Jingdezhen. Among the most important pieces in the collection are the approximately one hundred blue and white pieces dating to the Yuan Dynasty (when China was administered by Mongol rulers and blue and white porcelain was first made) and the early Ming Dynasty. An inscribed Vietnamese vase is also included.

Blue and white ewer, Qing Dynasty, China

The blue and white porcelains of the Ming Dynasty (1368-1644) reflect not only Chinese culture but also the cultures of the countries to which they were exported. It was at the beginning of the 16th century that products designed specifically for Muslims began to be produced.

During the Qing Dynasty (1644-1912), blue and white porcelain began to be produced in greater numbers but the quality gradually declined: what had been expensive products during the Yuan and Ming dynasties became cheaper and more accessible. The palace's collection contains 2,680 examples of blue and white porcelain from the Qing Dynasty. Among these are numerous varied pieces from the time of the Kangxi Emperor (r. 1661-1722).

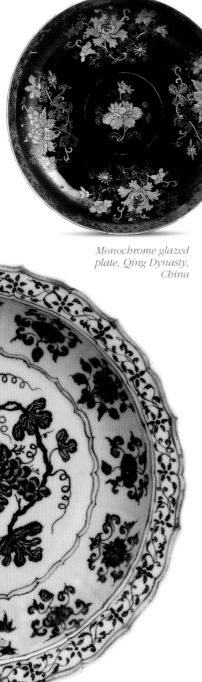

Monochromes

The palace collection includes 31 pieces of white porcelain; these, which date from the early 15th century, are decorated with either underglaze reliefs or scored embellishments. There is also a very small number of yellow porcelain bowls produced for China's imperial palace. How these pieces, which are glazed with "imperial yellow" and bear the imperial seal, came to be in Topkapı Palace remains unknown. However, it is thought that they may have either been official gifts or war plunder. As their colour resembles gold, they may also have been used by the sultans during the month of Ramadan. The collection also includes 53 glazed monochrome pieces fired at a low temperature and coloured in various tones of yellow, emerald green and iron red. Also found in the collection are 18th-century examples of Longquan monochrome porcelains featuring celadon glazing and scored embellishments.

Monochrome glazed plate, Qing Dynasty, China

Blue and white plate, early Ming Dynasty, China

Polychromes

In China, porcelains decorated with polychrome enamels were first produced and exported during the middle period of the Ming Dynasty but it was during the Qing Dynasty that they reached their zenith. The most important group of early Qing porcelains is the group known as Famille verte (Green variety). Green was dominant among this variety's enamel colours and the palace collection contains 226 examples of Famille verte porcelain as such. Another group was Famille rose (Pink variety), which were produced in the late Kangxi period using rose pink and matte white enamels and were exported in great quantities during the reigns of the emperors Yongzheng (r. 1722-35) and Qianlong (r. 1735-96). The palace collection contains 527 examples of Famille rose porcelain. A set of about 130 pieces of the second half of the 18th century, with enamel decorations and verses in gold leaf from the Qur'an inscribed within cartouches, makes up an important part of this collection.

Famille Rose bowl, Qing Dynasty, China

Famille Verte plate, Qing Dynasty, China

Japanese Porcelains

The Topkapı Palace Museum contains approximately 700 Japanese porcelains. Nearly the entire collection consists of pieces produced specifically for export in the town of Arita, on the northern part of the Japanese island of Kyushu. A large number of these pieces were transferred from Yıldız Palace (the residence of Sultan Abdülhamid II (r. 1876-1909)) to the Istanbul Museum of Ancient Artifacts (İstanbul Âsâr-ı Atîka, currently the Istanbul Archaeology Museum) and from there to the Topkapı Palace Museum in 1927.

The Imari blue and white porcelains have an important place in the palace collection. It was in the town of Arita that

Blue and white Ko-Imari ewer, Arita, Japan

the Kakiemon, Nabeshima, and Imari styles were developed based on enameling techniques imported from China in the middle of the 17th century. The Kakiemon style, which formed the basis of traditional Japanese porcelain, is represented in the palace collection by a single plate. The collection also features numerous pieces of Imari and Ko-Imari porcelain, most dated to the period between 1690 and 1740. In addition to these, the collection also features Kutani porcelains which were typically produced for export to Europe and in which brick red is the dominant colour; Hirado porcelains, noteworthy for their extremely fine glaze; late 19th-century examples of Seto ceramics, which had first gone into production in 1810; Satsuma bowls whose dominant colours are gold and red; and ceramics made in Arita and known by that name, produced during the Bakumatsu period (1853-1868).

△ *Japanese Imari lidded jar, Arita, Japan. Early 18th century*

▽ *Japanese Imari plate, Arita, Japan. 18th century*

CHINESE PORCELAINS

At the Edirne palace in 1457, Chinese porcelains were used during the banquet celebrating the circumcision of Sultan Mehmed II's sons, Bayezid and Mustafa. The first record of the use of Chinese porcelains at Topkapı Palace is found in a treasury inventory record of 1496, which mentions six porcelain pieces. From the 17th century to the early 18th century, the number of porcelains found in the palace steadily increased. When, in the time of Sultan Abdülmecid (r. 1839-1861), the imperial family relocated from Topkapı Palace to European-style palaces-first to Dolmabahçe Palace and later to Yıldız Palace. The relocation led to many different changes, among them a change in eating habits as members of the imperial family took on European habits such as eating from separate plates, sitting together around a dining table, and using forks and knives. The European porcelains found in the Topkapı Palace collections date from this period.

Miniature depicting a feast for high-ranking officers where Chinese porcelain was utilised. Levni, Surnâme (fol. 85b)

EUROPEAN PORCELAINS AND GLASSWARE

There are approximately 5,000 examples of porcelain ware produced in various countries in Europe in the palace collection. These pieces comprise German, French, Austrian, and Russian porcelains produced between the beginning of the 18th century and the beginning of the 20th century as well as faïence from Warsaw, Italy, and Spain. Among these works (an important part of which entered the palace collection by way of purchase transfer from Yıldız Palace) are many early period European porcelains sent to the sultan and to palace dignitaries as gifts of state. These pieces are especially striking for their fine craftsmanship.

German Porcelains

The first producer of porcelain in Germany was the chemist Johann Friedrich Böttger, who worked under the patronage of Augustus II the Strong, King of Poland and Elector of Saxony. The German porcelains in the Topkapı Palace collection comprise porcelains stamped as Meissen, Dresden, Höchst, Berlin, Frankenthal, and Nymphenburg.

Meissen porcelain holds an important place in German porcelain production. The palace collection includes examples of early Meissen porcelain, dated 1717. A second group of porcelains in the collection are the Berlin porcelains stamped as KPM. Among the collection's most beautiful pieces are a porcelain clock, dated 1857 and signed by Tallibart, and a pair of candelabra.

The third group of German porcelains in the collection are products of the Höchst porcelain factory which was located in the Principality of Mainz and began production in 1746. Porcelains produced in the Nymphenburg porcelain factory between 1769 and 1774 make up the fourth group of German porcelains in the palace collection.

Austrian Porcelains

Throughout the 18th century and in the first half of the 19th century, the porcelain factories of Meissen and Vienna put great care into ensuring that the porcelains they exported to the Ottoman Empire were produced in such a way as to accord with Ottoman traditions and customs. The pieces made for the Ottoman palace with this in mind include covered plates, trays, candy boxes and coffee kettles.

Among the oldest and most important of the Viennese porcelains in the palace collection are a basin and pitcher set and a dining service set produced in 1730.

French Porcelains

French porcelains are an important part of the European porcelain tradition. Production began between 1738 and 1756 at the Château de Vincennes near Paris. One of the most important pieces of French porcelain in the Topkapı

An early example of Du Paquier period Viennese porcelain. Basin and ewer, 18th century

French porcelain pair of lidded bowls bearing the calligraphic seal of Sultan Abdülmecid and a Turkish flag pattern, 1839–1861

Palace collection is a dining set decorated with a forest view which was produced in the time of Louis-Philippe, King of the French (r. 1830-1848).

One group among the collection's French porcelains comprises of pieces produced at the porcelain factory established in Limoges in 1770. Among these works is a statuette of a pair of pigeons, made in 1867 and signed by Comolera.

Also among the French porcelains are the products of private workshops such as Baschet & Frère, Brever Brianchon and Rousseau. These include two covered plates produced by Rousseau and decorated with the imperial seal of Sultan Abdülmecid (r. 1839-61) and a pattern of Turkish flags, several pitchers, glasses, plates, and bowls bearing the stamp of Jacob Petit (items which began to be produced in Paris in the 1820s). These pieces are among the finest examples of French porcelain in the palace collection.

Russian Porcelains

All of the Russian porcelains in the palace collection were produced in the time of Tsar Nicholas I (r. 1825-55) in the imperial porcelain factory in St. Petersburg. These porcelains were sent by Nicholas I to Sultan Mahmud II (r. 1808-39) as gifts of state (archival documents state that what was sent was a dining set consisting of 2,000 pieces). Currently, however, the collection comprises of approximately 450 pieces of Russian porcelain.

European Faïence

Of the palace collection's examples of European faïence (which includes pieces produced in Spain, France, and Germany) perhaps the finest is the dining set sent as a gift of state in October 1732 to Sultan Abdülhamid I by Stanislaw Poniatowski (later to be King and Grand Duke of the Polish-Lithuanian Commonwealth (r. 1764-95)).

Oval plate from the dining set sent to Sultan Abdülhamid I by Stanislaw Poniatowski, King and Grand Duke of the Polish-Lithuanian Commonwealth

This set was produced in imitation of Japanese Imari porcelain and the pieces are inscribed with words in praise of the sultan.

European Glassware

The palace's European glassware collection comprises of basin and pitcher sets, candy bowls, covered bowls, large and small plates, carafes and glasses, sherbet glasses and pitchers, coffee cups and holders, chandeliers and candelabra.

Bohemian glass and crystal make up an especially important part of the collection.

Beginning in the first half of the 17th century, a new variety of glass began to be manufactured in Bohemia using a technique that revolutionized the glassmaking industry. Among the works in this collection is a set consisting of a decanter and six glasses, produced expressly for Sultan Abdülhamid II (r.1876-1909) by Ludwig Moser, who worked at the Bohemia Glassworks between 1857 and 1893. The palace collection also includes French, English, and Russian glassware.

Gift sent to Sultan Mahmud II by the Russian Tsar Nicholas I

European glass pitcher and glasses with the inscription of Sultan Abdulhamid II

ISTANBUL GLASS AND PORCELAIN WARE

The Istanbul Glass and Porcelain Ware collection is made up of approximately 2,000 pieces, with a large part of the collection being exhibited in the palace kitchens and in the Sherbet Chamber (Şerbethâne) and the Confectionery House (Helvâhâne), which are connected to one another.

The production of glass in Istanbul began with the Mevlevi dervish Mehmet Dede who was sent to Italy by Sultan Selim III (r. 1789-1807) to learn glassmaking techniques. Having studied these techniques in Venice, he returned to Istanbul, where he began making glass pieces that, though at first resembling the glass products of Venice, soon began to show a distinct Istanbul style. In the glass workshops that were founded in Beykoz and that became synonymous with Istanbul glassmaking from the 19th century onwards, three different techniques were used: "çeşm-i Bülbül" (eye of the nightingale)

*Beykoz-ware glass snow cooler
with çeşm-i bülbül pattern,
19th century*

*Beykoz-ware glass carafe with
çeşm-i bülbül pattern, 19th century*

glass; opaline glass; and crystal and transparent glass. Of these, it is "çeşm-i Bülbül" glass (in which coloured sticks of glass are bound with the body of the glass piece and then twisted) that is most identified with Beykoz glass.

The Ottoman porcelains in the collection, highly valuable and thus designed exclusively for use in the palace, can be classed into two separate groups: those branded as "Eser-i İstanbul" (Product of Istanbul) and Yıldız porcelains. The Eser-i İstanbul porcelains were the first Ottoman porcelains to be produced, beginning production in the time of Sultan Abdülmecid (r. 1839-61) in the workshops of Beykoz. The porcelain objects made in these workshops were produced using the underglaze technique and bear the "Eser-i İstanbul" brand on their bottoms. The colour of the paints used to decorate the piece are typically the same as the colour found in the brand. The production of Eser-i İstanbul porcelains, which are distinguished by their patterns of large flowers, lasted just thirty years before production was ended due to ongoing financial difficulties.

Yıldız porcelains comprise the second group of Ottoman porcelains. Production began in 1890, in the time of Sultan Abdülhamid II (r.1876-1909), in a factory established in the garden of Yıldız Palace. The name of the factory was the Imperial Yıldız Factory of Chinaware (Yıldız Çini Fabrika-ı Hümâyûn). Porcelains

Yıldız-ware porcelain vase, 19th century

Yıldız-ware porcelain coffee cups bearing portraits of Sultan Murad IV and Sultan Abdülmecid, end of 19th century

produced here were marked with the crescent and star symbol and the year of manufacture. One important detail of the Yıldız porcelains is that some of them are inscribed with the name of the artist who created them. These porcelains are decorated with floral patterns, traditional Ottoman motifs, landscapes, pictures of historical structures, portraits of the sultan, the calligraphic seal of

Yıldız porcelain wall plate with an illustration of Selim III

Yıldız porcelain wall plate with an illustration of Mahmud II

Yıldız-ware porcelain clock, 19th century

Yıldız porcelain Jewellery box (with scenes from the Çinili Kiosk and the Topkapı Palace), late 19th century

Sultan Abdülhamid II, pictures of palace women and children and various animal designs. The porcelains decorated with Istanbul landscapes and pictures of historical structures today have a very high archival value. Though the Yıldız porcelains were primarily produced to satisfy the need for porcelain of the palace residents, they were also given as gifts to foreign statesmen and high-level Ottoman dignitaries. Additionally, Yıldız porcelains were sent to the kings, queens, tsars, and tsarinas of Europe as gifts of state and can still be found in European palaces today, albeit in small numbers.

The third group of works in the Istanbul Glass and Porcelain Ware collection comprises of ceramic objects made of meerschaum. These ceramics were produced in Istanbul's Tophane neighborhood, and thus called Tophane Works. Being of rather high quality and prestige, they were a type of ceramic used by palace residents and high-level dignitaries.

Helvahâne

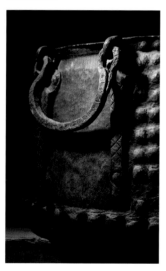

COPPER AND BRASS WORKS

Copper works, an important part of Topkapı Palace's kitchenware, are exhibited in the Confectionery House (Helvahâne) where sweets such as halva, candies, the gumlike candy called "macun", "baklava", many other confections and also soap were produced for the use of the palace residents.

All of the pots used to cook food in the palace kitchens are made entirely of copper. These pots are quite big, since they were used to serve all those resident in the palace. This would amount to food for at least five thousand people per day and even more on special occasions. The collection includes copper pots with diameters of 60, 70, and 105 centimeters. Copper pots meant for use in Topkapı Palace were produced in Istanbul's Süleymaniye district. The hammering technique was used in the construction of the pots, while chasing and incising were used in their decoration.

Tombac ware is an important group within the palace's kitchenware. Tombac, obtained by applying a gold and

Tombac basin and ewer. End of 18th century

Tombac tray. 18th century

Tombac basin and ewer. Mid 18th century

mercury alloy to copper so as to produce a golden hue, was first used in Ottoman culture in the 16th century but did not achieve widespread use until the 17th century. Several examples of tombac ware dating from the 18th and 19th centuries can be found in the palace collection: basin and ewer sets, rose water vessels (gülâbdan), censers, containers for cups and for sherbet, water jugs, milk pitchers, small service trays, covered bowls, soup bowls, coffee kettles, ladles and containers for carrying cooked food. Additionally, the collection contains stone kitchen bowls, marble and bronze mortars, small plates made of coloured stone, service trays, candy bowls, and sherbet glasses.

Rose water vessel.
18th century

Talisman engraved copper bath bowl. 18th century

Talisman engraved copper bath bowl. 18th century

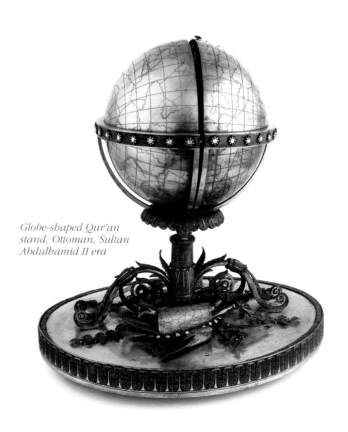

Globe-shaped Qur'an stand, Ottoman, Sultan Abdulhamid II era

OTTOMAN AND EUROPEAN SILVERWARE

The rich collection of silverware in the Topkapı Palace Museum, made up of works from the 16th to the 19th centuries, constitutes an important part of the Ottoman Empire treasury. Consisting of approximately 2,000 works in silver, the collection contains pieces transferred from the palace treasury, gifts received by the sultans on the occasion of their accession to the throne, works brought to the sultan by visiting European diplomats, as well as pieces that were obtained by means of donation or purchase.

The oldest dated work in the collection is a round tray bearing the calligraphic seal of Sultan Suleiman the Magnificent (r. 1520-66). The collection's 16th- and 17th-century works in silver represent perhaps the greatest examples of Ottoman metalworking. The Ottoman taste and style of that era are reflected in the silver basin and pitcher sets, braziers, plates, bird cages, bowls, and candy and tea sets. From the 18th century onwards, the influence of European silver working and decorative styles become increasingly apparent, particularly the influence of French silver working.

*Silver Brazier.
19th century*

*Basin and
ewer, Ottoman.
1840*

Silver dressing table

One noteworthy part of the collection are the works in silver presented to Sultan Abdülhamid II (r. 1876-1909) on the silver jubilee, or twenty-fifth anniversary, of his accession to the throne. Among these works are those produced by jewelry workshops on special request including vases, a dressing table with mirror, models of the Fountain of Sultan Ahmed III, of the İzmir Clock Tower, of the ship Şükran and of the Obelisk of Theodosius, which stands in İstanbul's Hippodrome (Sultanahmet Meydanı).

A particularly interesting and important work in the collection is the silver flask. During the 1901 opening ceremony of the German Fountain in the Hippodrome, some water from the fountain was placed into a large silver flask, the flask's beak was sealed, and the flask was sent to the German Emperor Wilhelm II. There were, however, two of these silver flasks, with the second being presented to Sultan Abdülhamid II; this is the flask now found in the collection.

WEAPONRY

The weaponry used by the Ottoman army was manufactured in various workshops and stored in armories called "cebehâne" where their maintenance and repairs would also be done. The first Ottoman "cebehâne" was established in Edirne. Following the conquest of Constantinople, Sultan Mehmed II converted the Church of Hagia Eirene in Topkapı Palace's First Courtyard into a cebehâne, for which purpose this building would continue to be used until the late 19th century. In 1846, at the initiative of Fethi Ahmed Pasha, the Commander of the Cannon Foundry (Tophâne), the Church of Hagia Eirene was reorganized so as to form Turkey's first museum, "The Collection of Ancient Weapons and the Collection of Antiquities" (Mecma`-ı Esliha-ı `Atîka ve Mecma`-ı Âsâr-ı `Atîka). The museum's weaponry was kept here until Topkapı Palace began to be used as a museum in the early 20th century. These weapons would later form the basis of the Military Museum's collection, which is among the richest such collections in the world.

Covering 1,300 years and consisting of 52,000 weapons of Arab, Umayyad, Abbasid, Mamluk, Persian, Turkish, Crimean Tatar, Indian, European and Japanese origins, the Topkapı Palace Museum's weaponry collection is also among the world's premier weapons collections. The collection is made up in part of

Sword Ottoman Empire, second half of the 15th century. The grip of the sword, which belonged to Sultan Mehmed the Conqueror, is made of fish teeth. There is a two-lined calligraphic inscription in the thuluth style on one of the sides of the sharp blade of the sword.

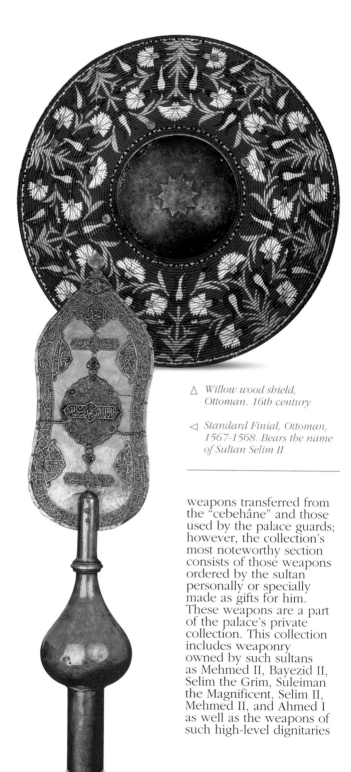

△ *Willow wood shield, Ottoman. 16th century*

◁ *Standard Finial, Ottoman, 1567-1568. Bears the name of Sultan Selim II*

weapons transferred from the "cebehâne" and those used by the palace guards; however, the collection's most noteworthy section consists of those weapons ordered by the sultan personally or specially made as gifts for him. These weapons are a part of the palace's private collection. This collection includes weaponry owned by such sultans as Mehmed II, Bayezid II, Selim the Grim, Süleiman the Magnificent, Selim II, Mehmed II, and Ahmed I as well as the weapons of such high-level dignitaries

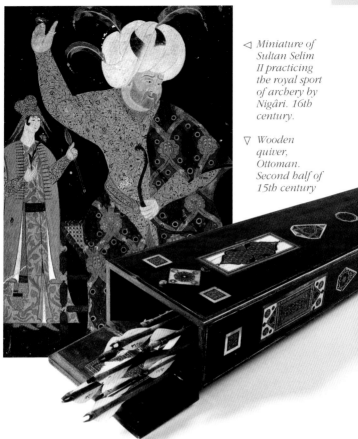

◁ Miniature of Sultan Selim II practicing the royal sport of archery by Nigâri. 16th century.

▽ Wooden quiver, Ottoman. Second half of 15th century

as grand viziers, pashas, and palace chamberlains; all of these weapons are eye-catching with their fine craftsmanship and decorations. An additional factor that contributed to the diversification of the collection's highly artistic weaponry was the tradition of bringing the weapons of important figures that were obtained through plunder to the palace.

The collection's earliest pieces are the swords of Umayyad and Abbasid caliphs, dating from the 7th to the 13th centuries, and Mamluk weapons of the 14th to 16th centuries, such as swords, helmets, armor, banners, and halberds. Among the weapons brought to the palace as plunder following Sultan Selim the Grim's conquest of Egypt in 1517 are weapons that had been owned by such Mamluk sultans as Qaitbay (r. 1468-96) and Qansuh al-Ghawri (r. 1501-16). These are weapons that not only reflect the technology of their time, but that also have a very high artistic value. The Persian weapons that were brought to the palace

▷ *Bow Case (Tirkeş)
Ottoman. 16th century*

---

consists of bows, swords,
halberds, lances, banners,
armor, and helmets.
While these Mamluk and
Persian weapons reflect the
diversity, fine craftsmanship,
and decorative taste of
Islamic metalworking, the
collection also contains
various examples of

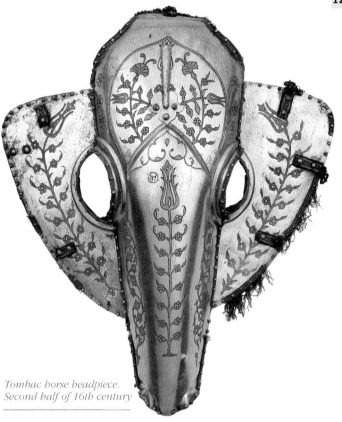

Tombac horse headpiece.
Second half of 16th century

European weaponry obtained by plunder, as well as Crimean Tartar, Indian, and Japanese weapons presented as gifts.

The richest part of the collection, both in number and variety, is the Ottoman weaponry. The bow and arrow was the most characteristic weapon of the Ottoman army, and continued to be used after the introduction of firearms. From the 16th century to the end of the 19th century, the bow and arrow were also used as a sport. The collection also contains bows made by Sultan Bayezid II. Other Ottoman weapons in the collection include piercing weapons such as lances and javelins which are known to have been used since the very earliest times. Cutting weapons such as swords, yataghans (a type of curved sword), rapiers, scimitars, daggers, stilettos, Yemeni daggers, battle axes, and halberds and items designed to protect against piercing and cutting weapons, such as helmets, shields, armour, and horse armour are also to be found. Armour was not much used by the Ottoman army, owing to the fact that it restricted movement. Unlike the knights of Europe, Ottoman soldiers would not wear armor from head to toe, preferring to

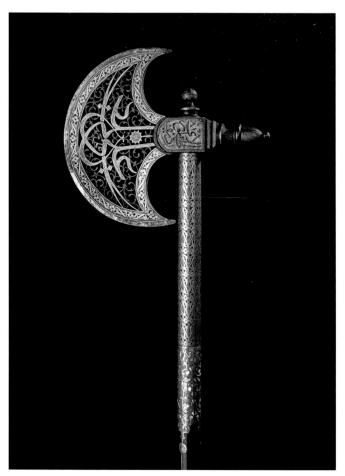

Battle Axe, 18th century

cover only those parts of the body that were most vulnerable.

Another important part of the weaponry collection consists of firearms, including rifles from the 16th century onwards and pistols from the 18th century onwards. These weapons reflect the historical development of firearms with their fuse-, flint-, or capsule-based firing mechanisms, as well as being reflective of the decorative styles of their particular period and of the regional patterns and tastes of such places as Istanbul, the Caucasus, and the Balkans. Apart from piercing weapons, cutting weapons, defensive items and firearms, the palace collection also includes blunt instruments such as maces, war-clubs and such symbols of sovereignty as horsetail plumes, regimental colours and banners and wooden shields with metal

Helmet, Ottoman, 16th century

centres (söğüt kalkan).
Nearly all of the weapons used in the Ottoman Empire were fine examples of craftsmanship and ornamentation. The metal parts of such weapons as swords, daggers, rapiers, shields, helmets, armor, rifles, and pistols would very often be worked with floral-patterned gold and silver inlays, reliefs, or engravings, within which would be inscribed verses from the Qur'an, poetic inscriptions or the name of the piece's craftsman or owner. The wooden parts of bows and arrows would be decorated with drawings or lacquered while the wooden parts of such weapons as swords, rifles, and pistols would be embellished by bone, ivory, gold, or silver appliqué or inlay; such decorative touches would also at times have the added flourish of precious or semi-precious stones.

SULTANS' CLOTHES

The collection of sultans' clothing, which showcases perhaps the finest examples of Ottoman textile art, contains clothing of the sultans and princes from the second half of the 15th century to the early 20th century. The collection was assembled owing to the tradition of bundling together all the garments worn by recently deceased sultans and princes, labeling them, and then storing them in the palace treasury. The collection has also been enriched by the addition of the caftans, turbans, and coverings placed on the sarcophagi of sultans and others in the Ottoman dynasty.

In the Ottoman Empire, clothing was not merely functional or aesthetic, but also served as a symbol of the wearer's professional, ethnic, and social status. As such, measures were taken by means of various regulations to determine and preserve the clothing

The ceremonial robe of Prince Korkud,
Ottoman Empire. Second half of the 15th century

styles of different social groups. Ottoman clothing thus served as an essential element in official ceremonies showcasing the empire's cultural identity, as well its ideology of power and sovereignty.

One of the collection's earliest pieces is the ceremonial caftan with turndown collar that belonged to Prince Korkud (d.1513), son of Sultan Bayezid II (r. 1481-1512). This caftan is made of Italian velvet, and has an appliqué decorative pattern as well as a very striking lining. There are numerous caftans of Italian velvet in the collection of the Topkapı Palace Museum which clearly reflects the taste of the Ottoman sultans and princes for Italian silk. The fact that Italian silk was so highly valued and generally preferred may well have been due to the fine patterns and compositions found on this fabric, as well as its red and gold hues.

The palace collection also contains many inner caftans. These are typically uncollared, tight-fitting, short-sleeved garments open at the front; they had slits along the side stitches of the skirt and widened below the waist by means of pieces of fabric added

to the garment's front and side apertures. Closing from right to left, the inner caftans also have strip-shaped front fasteners called "çaprast". Some of the short-sleeved inner caftans would be made of the same fabric as the outer caftan, and the sleeves would be attached to the outer caftan by means of buttons on their upper part.

The outer and inner caftans were worn over a loose inner robe called

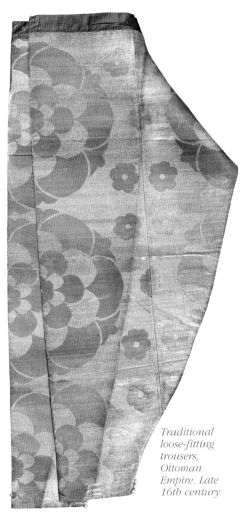

Traditional loose-fitting trousers, Ottoman Empire. Late 16th century

"entari", which were long-sleeved garments open in front, with silk-threaded buttons extending down to the waist.

In the empire's early period, the caftan and "entari" had contrasting colours, but identical colours became common beginning in the second half of the 18th century. Apart from these garments, the Ottoman sultans would also wear traditional wide-stitch shalwar trousers which had separate legs pleated on the upper part and whose wide waist would be drawn in by a sash passed through drawstrings on the waistband.

When the sultans would appear before the public during ceremonies, they would typically wear a type of brocade known as "serâser", woven with gold and silver thread and visually expressive of their power and majesty: the silk yarn found in "serâser" cloth was made in Bursa while its gold and silver wire was manufactured in special workshops called "sîmkeşhâne". Production of serâser cloth, which was typically woven with patterns of large dimensions, began in Istanbul in the 16th century. Currently, the palace collection contains only those few garments of serâser cloth that have survived.

◁ *Ceremonial robe*
Ottoman Empire, mid. 16th
century or the third quarter
of 16th century

▽ *Robe*
Ottoman Empire, late 16th
century- early 17th century

The decorative patterns of the sultans' clothing were drawn up by palace miniaturists, who made up a large part of the court's artists and artisans working for the court, or "ehl-i hiref". Besides "serâser" cloth, the sultans' garments were made with expensive silks such as velvet, "çatma" velvet (with raised designs) and "kemha" or velvet pile. Beginning in the time of Sultan Ahmed III (r. 1703-30), these heavy and expensive fabrics (due to their large amount of gold and silver thread) were replaced with lighter and simpler fabrics such as satin, taffeta, "gezi" (thickly woven silk cloth), "canfes" (thin taffeta), "sandal" (a mixture of cotton and silk), geremsut silk, and "selimiye" (silk cloth made in workshops near İstanbul's Selimiye barracks).

The robe and the brassards of Suleiman the Magnificent.
Ottoman Empire, 1550

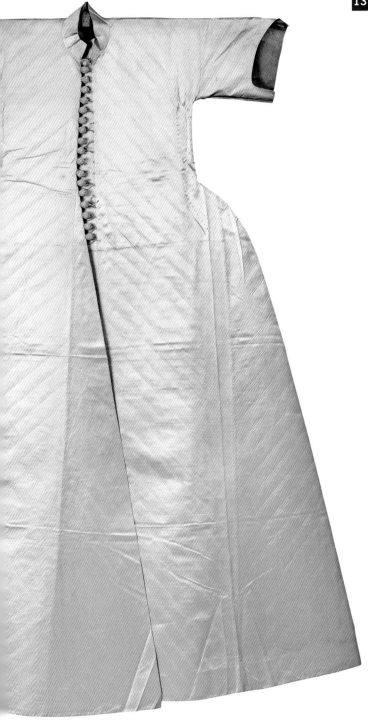

For the Ottoman sultans, headgear not only completed an outfit, but also served as an important status symbol. During ceremonies and on reception days, sultans would wear headgear called "horasanî", "mücevveze", "selimî", or "kâtibî". Sultan Mehmed II (r. 1451-81) and Sultan Bayezid II (r. 1481-1512) are known to have worn the mücevveze, a red-topped cylindrical turban widening towards the top and with a height of 32-33 centimetres; the "mücevveze" would be prepared by wrapping white muslin around cardboard. The muslin-covered turban type known as "selimî" (so named because it was first used by Sultan Selim the Grim (r. 1512-20)) also had a cylindrical shape, with a relatively wider top than the bottom part resting on the head. In addition to the "selimî", the flat-topped "kâtibî turban" came into use in the time of Sultan Ahmed III (r. 1703-30).

Another important piece of Ottoman headgear was the fez. In 1827, Sultan Mahmud II issued an imperial decree

◁ *Quilted Turban of the Scribes. Ottoman Empire, late 17th century-early 18th century*

▽ *The armored Kaftan of Sultan Mehmed the Conqueror. Ottoman Empire, 1470*

TALISMANIC SHIRTS

On the talismanic shirts found in the Sultans' Clothing collection are written verses from the Qur'an and various prayers which was believed to protect the wearer from illnesses and enemies. There were even claims that these talismanic shirts could protect the wearer from swords and bullets.

Apart from the Qur'anic verses and prayers on the shirts, there are also various geometric shapes, pictures of the Kaaba in Mecca, and floral patterns reminiscent of those used as ornamentation for books; all of these were drawn primarily in black and red ink with gilding and silvering used as the base. The talismanic shirts were most likely prepared through a collaborative effort between astrologers and theologians.

The writing on the talismanic shirt belonging to Cem Sultan, son of Sultan Mehmed II (r.1451-81), began and ended on an hour indicated by astrologers as being particularly auspicious and known as "eşref-i sâ`at."

This shirt can currently be seen in the palace collection.

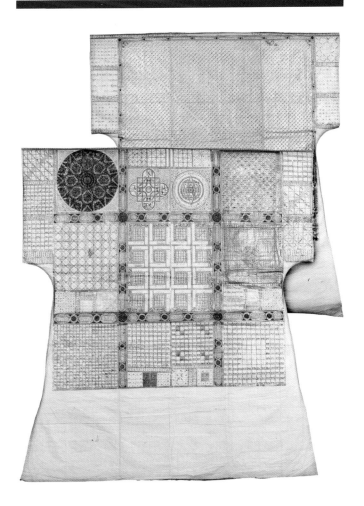

Ceremonial Uniform (jacket and trousers) worn by Sultan Murad V at his enthronement ceremony in 1876

abolishing the Janissary corps and establishing a new army called the "Asâkir-i Mansûre-i Muhammediye" (Victorious Soldiers of Muhammad), whose mandatory uniform consisted not only of coat and trousers, but also of the fez. Subsequently, a new clothing regulation was introduced obliging all state employees and religious scholars to wear the fez. This clothing reform of Sultan Mahmud II served as a means of promotion for the radical changes he brought to the structure of the Ottoman state. The introduction of the fez resulted in other kinds of headgear losing their function as status symbols.

THE IMPERIAL TREASURY

The sultans would observe the items in the treasury as if taking part in a special ceremony. In addition to being great works of art, the items also have great historical, monetary, and spiritual value. Since the treasury was, in effect, a memento of the royal family, the sultans showed special care in enriching its collection. The items in the treasury were originally kept in chests and cupboards that would only be opened on the occasion of the sultans' visitation. It was Sultan Abdülmecid (r. 1839-61) who broke this tradition by putting some of the objects on display; this continued in the time of Sultan Abdülaziz (r. 1861-76) and Sultan Abdülhamid II (r. 1876-1909).

That tradition continues today as the valuable objects belonging to the Ottoman sultans are now on display in the palace's Imperial Treasury section (Hazîne-i Hümâyûn).

Following the conversion of Topkapı Palace into a museum in 1924, the treasury objects were classified and used as the basis of the museum's collections.

A large part of the palace treasury is made up of gifts presented at ambassadorial receptions and gifts presented on the occasion of the sultans' weddings, of births, and of the circumcision festivities of the princes. While such gifts as these would sometimes be brought to the sultan from the four corners of the world, other gifts would be presented by local artists and artisans who would, in exchange for their gifts, receive not only gifts in return, but also promises of support and future purchase of their works. The sultans would also, on occasion, send gifts to foreign rulers; however, for various reasons, some of these would not reach their destination, in which case they would be returned and take their place in the palace treasury. An example of this sort of gift is the emerald dagger and emerald- and diamond-studded bow and quivers sent by Sultan Mahmud I (r. 1730-54).

Among the other works found in the palace treasury are the precious objects of state dignitaries which were requisitioned for the treasury upon their owners' deaths, and plundered objects. Among the finest of these plundered objects are

PENDANTS, PLUMES

Jewelled pendants were decorative elements used on thrones, on the domes or ceilings of the sultan's rooms and on the doors of entrances through which the sultan would pass. Additionally, there were pendants made for the tomb of the Prophet Mohammad in Medina. The pendants commissioned by Sultan Ahmed I (r. 1603-17), Sultan Mustafa III (r. 1757-74), Sultan Abdülhamid I (r. 1774-89), Sultan Selim III (r. 1789-1807), Sultan Mahmud II (r. 1808-39), and Sultan Abdülmecid (r. 1839-61) can be recognized by the calligraphic seals and inscriptions found on them.

Plumes were perhaps the most important jewels worn by Ottoman sultans and princes. These gold objects bearing emeralds, rubies, diamonds, or pearls would be fastened to turbans together with fine bird feathers. State dignitaries also wore plumes, but more modest versions. Some of the palace's plumes have remained in the museum's collection.

◁ *Emerald Pendant*
*On the lid of the pendant,
the name of Sultan
Mustafa III (reign: 1757-
1774) is inscribed. The
golden piece holding
together the 38 strings
of pearl is adorned with
diamonds. The pendant
was made for the tomb of
Muhammad the Prophet
in Medina.*

▽ *Bejeweled Crest*
*As a whole, the crest which is
encrusted with gold, diamonds,
rubies and emeralds, looks like a
tulip. Its chains are embellished
with rubies, diamonds and
teardrop-shaped emeralds. This
artwork, constituting one of the
major examples of 18th century
crest craftsmanship, has a
golden slot for feathers wherein
the feather of the Huma or the
Bird of Paradise is seated.*

the belt, armband, and drinking cup of the Safavid ruler Shah Ismail I (r. 1502-24)as well as various metal works of the early Safavid period, such as zinc vessels.

Additionally, one important group of objects in the treasury is made up of objects brought from Yıldız Palace following the declaration of the Republic of Turkey.

A particularly important place in the treasury is held by those items originally sent to Medina by the sultans for the tomb of the Prophet Muhammad.

Among these items, the most noteworthy are the gold and glass oil lamp made on the order of Sultan Murad III (r. 1574-95) and the solid gold candelabrum decorated with diamonds and an inscription and made on the order of Sultan Abdülmecid. The enamel-on-gold censer and rosewater vessel sent by Abdülmecid's daughter Cemile Sultan are also among these works which were returned to the treasury for protection during the First World War by Fahrettin Pasha, the commander in the Hejaz region.

Golden Candlesticks made for the tomb of Muhammad the Prophet upon the order of Sultan Abdulmecid. These solid gold candlesticks, each of which weighs 48 kilograms are encrusted with hundreds of brilliants

Festival Eve Throne of Sultan Ahmed I

The most important items in the Imperial Treasury are the thrones, which are on display in the treasury's first room. The Festivity Throne (Bayram Tahtı) (made of walnut wood, covered with panels of solid gold, and encrusted with chrysolite) was used on occasions attended by the sultan. Among these occassions, the most noteworthy are accession to the throne and holiday festivities; this throne corresponds to the description of a golden throne found in records of the 16th century.

The Throne of the Eve (Arife Tahtı) of Sultan Ahmed I (r. 1603-17) is a unique example of Ottoman mother-of-pearl inlay. Made of walnut wood and ornamented with tortoiseshell, mother-of-pearl, and precious stones, this throne is the work of the architect Mehmed Agha who spent much time doing mother-of-pearl inlay work. Another throne found here is the ebony throne used by Sultan Murad IV (r. 1623-40) in his Baghdad campaign of 1638. Similar in form to the Festivity Throne, it has inlay of mother-of-pearl and ivory. There is also a wooden throne with enameled and gem-studded gold panels which was sent to Sultan Mahmud I as a diplomatic gift by Nadir Shah of Persia.

The structure of the throne and the manner in which its gems have been worked show that it was made in India under the Mughal Dynasty during the 18th century.

Although most of the works currently in the treasury date from the 16th to the 19th century, there are also objects of Byzantine, Mamluk, and Seljuk origin. Among these are the skull and the hand and arm bones of Saint John the Baptist, inherited from the Byzantines and kept in bejeweled cases; Mamluk oil lamps from the 14th century and the Seljuk sandal wood cabinet of Timur's grandson Uluğ Bey, which is inscribed and is a masterpiece of woodcarving.

Golden Festival Throne. This walnut-wood festival throne weighing 250 kg. is covered with thick golden plaques

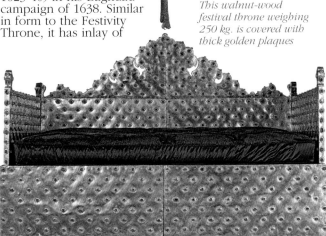

Treasury Weapons

The weapons in the treasury consist of swords, daggers, scimitars, yataghans, bows and quivers, thumb rings (zehgîr), helmets, pistols, heavy rifles and maces. Among these weapons, all uniformly decorated with precious stones, are a number of especially noteworthy items: the inscribed dagger of Sultan Selim the Grim (r. 1512-20), with its quartz-studded handle; the finely worked and inscribed metal yataghan of Sultan Suleiman the Magnificent (r. 1520-66), which bears the master craftsman's signature; a pistol presented as a gift by the German Emperor Wilhelm II (r. 1888-1918) and the armor of Sultan Mustafa III (r. 1757-74).

Sultan Mustafa III's suit of armor, 1771

THE SPOONMAKER'S DIAMOND (KAŞIKÇI ELMASI)

The Spoonmaker's Diamond is the largest and most famous of the historical diamonds in the Imperial Treasury. This 86-carat, pear-shaped diamond is surrounded by 49 brilliant-cut diamonds. Several diamond experts have attempted to prove that the Spoonmaker's Diamond is the historical Pigot Diamond, which was lost at the beginning of the 19th century; however, it is known from a record in a daily accounts book (rûznâme) that the diamond entered the Imperial Treasury by way of purchase at the beginning of the 1680s.

Several stories have circulated as to how the Spoonmaker's Diamond came to be in the palace. The most widely accepted among these is that recounted in the work Zübde-i Vak`aiyât (Summation of Events) by Sarı Mehmed Pasha, treasurer in the time of Sultan Mehmed IV (r. 1648-87). In this work, Mehmed Pasha describes the finding of the Spoonmaker's Diamond during the course of events in the year 1090 (May 1679):

"A round stone was found among the rubbish in the district of Eğrikapı and [brought to an] ironmonger, who exchanged the stone for three spoons and left it there among his items. Subsequently, one of the jewelers to whom the stone was shown purchased it for 10 akçe and showed the stone to one of his colleagues. When it was understood that the stone was, in fact, a diamond, the colleague also requested a share in the stone. A dispute then arose between the jeweler and his colleague and the situation was brought to the attention of the head jeweler, who gave to both jewelers a small purse full of akçe and took the stone off their hands. Subsequently, His Eminence the Grand Vizier Mustafa Pasha was made aware of the stone's existence and decided to obtain it from the head jeweler; however, when the situation was brought to the attention of the sultan, he commanded the stone to be brought to the palace. In summary, the stone was uncovered, ascertained to be an unparalleled diamond of the size of 84 carats and finally taken into the possession of the sultan. As a result, the head jeweler was rewarded with the office of gatekeeper as well as with a number of small purses of akche."

Gifts For The Sultans

Among the gifts that were sent to the sultans are a throne made in India; two small enameled statuettes decorated with precious stones and sent by the Mughals of India to Sultan Abdülaziz (r. 1861-76) while he was still a prince; a jeweled sword sent by Muzaffara'd-Din Shah Qajar of Persia to Sultan Abdülhamid II on the occasion of the latter's silver jubilee on 31 August 1901; a jade Fabergé vessel with jewelled coat of arms sent by the Russian Tsar Nicholas II (r. 1894-1917); a ewer, basin, and table sent from France; and an ebony walking stick ornamented with diamonds sent as a gift by the Mughals.

The Topkapı Dagger
The handle and the case of the dagger are made of gold. The handle is ornamented with three big emerald stones as well as a London-made watch. The emerald lid of the watch is also framed with diamonds. The dagger was sent to the Persian ruler Nader Shah as a gift by Sultan Mahmud I. Upon Nader Shah's death, the Ottoman mission brought the dagger and other gifts back to the palace.

Ceremonial gold flask decorated with jade threading, rubies and emeralds, c. 1560

Rock crystal writing set decorated with rubies and emeralds, 16th century. The interior of this box is covered in engraved golden plaques

The Ceremonial Flask

One important collection in the treasury are the Ottoman-made quartz flasks, water pitchers, rosewater vessels and boxes dating to the 16th and 17th centuries and decorated with gold and precious stones. Also, from the same time, are Persian, Indian, Chinese, and Ottoman jade vessels. In addition to these, there is a gold ceremonial flask that is perhaps the most noteworthy example of classic Ottoman jewellery and gold working: made of solid gold and decorated with precious stones, it was used in the times of Sultan Selim II (r. 1566-74) and Sultan Murad III (r. 1574-95).

THE CHAMBER OF THE HOLY RELICS

The Privy Room (Has Oda) was constructed in the Inner Courtyard in the time of Sultan Mehmed II (r. 1451-81) to serve as the private apartments of the sultan for which purpose it was used until the middle of the 16th century. Prior to their accession to the throne, the sultans would come to this room to pray and receive homage from the Privy Room officials before leaving for the ceremony.

On the walls of this two-storey structure of four basic spaces are found high-quality İznik tiles dating to the second half of the 16th century. The silver lattice on which the throne stands in the Privy Room dates to the time of Sultan Murad IV (r. 1623-40).

*The Holy Beard and its reliquary.
16th century*

The Chamber of the Holy Relics, located within the Privy Room, contains religious objects sent to the Ottoman sultans at various times between Sultan Selim the Grim's assumption of the caliphate in the 16th century to the end of the 19th century. The caliphate passed from the Abbasids to the Ottomans with Selim's conquest of Mamluk Egypt in 1517, upon which event the Holy Mantle of the Prophet (Hırka-i Saâdet) was given to Selim by al-Mutawakkil III: the last Abbasid caliph. The dispatching of holy relics to Istanbul would continue thereafter, particularly during the period of increasing Wahhabi assaults on holy places and objects in the late 18th and the 19th century when such objects were gradually removed to the Chamber of the Holy Relics for greater protection. Similarly, the holy objects found in Medina were sent to Topkapı Palace for the same reason during the First World War.

Among the most important holy relics to be collected in this way between the 16th century and the first half of the 20th century were the Holy Mantle of the Prophet; the hair from the Prophet's beard; the reliquary in which was kept the Prophet's tooth, broken during the Battle of Uhud on 19 March 625; and the footprints, letters, bow, and sword of the Prophet. There are also holy relics attributed to other prophets and to the companions of the Prophet Muhammad: the tray used by Abraham; the staff of Moses; the

View of the Chamber of the Holy Mantle as seen from the Petition Room

*Golden chest where the Prophet's sacred mantle is preserved.
Ottoman Empire, 19th century*

---

sword of David; the robe of Joseph; the swords of the Prophet Muhammad's companions; and the shirt, mantle, praying mat, and chest of Muhammad's daughter Fatimah.

In their office as Caliph of Islam, it was the duty of the Ottoman sultans to maintain and repair the Kaaba in Mecca, providing and renovating golden chandeliers, censers, rosewater vessels, oil lamps, supports and copies of the Qur'an. As these precious objects were replaced over time, they would be brought to Topkapı Palace and the current collection of holy relics includes some of them. Additionally, the collection includes items commissioned for the Kaaba by the sultans,

among them the Kaaba's gutters, keys, gates, and the reliquaries for the Black Stone (al-Hajaru'l-Aswad), the Holy Mantle, and the Holy Beard.

Also in the collection are models of the Mosque of the Prophet in Medina and the Dome of the Rock in Jerusalem; bottles of water from the Well of Zamzam made of white opal and sealed with red wax; soil from the field at Karbala; panels inscribed with Qur'anic verses; stands for the Qur'an; silver bowels; prayer rugs; censers used in the Privy Room and silver-handled brooms.

Every year on the 13th and 14th days of the month of Ramadan, the Ottoman sultans would personally

Silver case for storing the Honoured Standard. 17th century

Interior and exterior reliquaries for Muhammad the Prophet's tooth

*Sword of David
the Prophet,
10th century BC*

take part in the cleaning
of the objects and tiles
found in the Privy Room
with rose water dampened
sponges. Should the sultan
be ill or away on campaign
on these days, he would
appoint a deputy to take
his place in this duty. Once
this cleaning had been
completed, the sultan and
important state officials
would pay a formal visit
to the Holy Mantle of the
Prophet on the 15th day of
Ramadan.

The practice of the
forty aghas of the Privy
Room continuously reciting

Seal and its case belonging to the Prophet. Ottoman Empire, 19th century

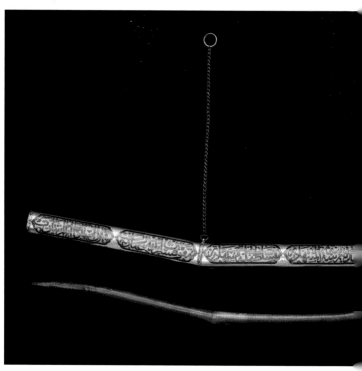

The Prophet's bow and its golden case.
7th century, Ottoman Empire, Sultan Ahmed I (1603-1617)

Prophet's letter of invitation to Islam addressed and sent to Muqawqis leader of the Copts

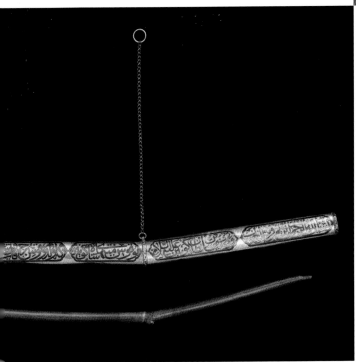

the Qur'an twenty-four hours a day, before the Holy Mantle of the Prophet began when Sultan Selim the Grim had the mantle brought to the Privy Room. This practice continued when the palace was converted into a museum under the auspices of the Republic of Turkey and is currently carried out in the first section of the Treasury of the Chamberlain by "hafiz" (those who have completely memorized the Qur'an) appointed by the Presidency of Religious Affairs (Diyanet İşleri Başkanlığı).

Wing of the Door of Repentance, Abbasid Caliphate, 1592

PORTRAITS OF SULTANS

Portraits of the Ottoman sultans comprise a part of the painting collection of the Topkapı Palace Museum. This collection is extremely valuable and contains a variety of portraits of the 36 different ruling sultans beginning with the foundation of the Ottoman state in 1299. These portraits are done in many different styles. Among them are engravings, oil paintings, watercolours and paintings on ivory.

No Ottoman sultan commissioned a portrait prior to Sultan Mehmed II (r. 1441-46, 1451-81); for this reason, portraits of the six sultans who ruled before this time were done either according to descriptions of the sultans found in historical texts or were entirely imagined. Most of the sultans who assumed the throne after Mehmed II commissioned portraits of themselves. Those portraits done according to the style of the miniatures tradition by artists working in the miniatures workshop of the palace reflect the physical characteristics of each sultan in a highly realistic manner. The most important factor in this realism was the fact that the artists who did these portraits, most of which were commissioned by the sultans themselves, had the opportunity to see the sultan up close and personal. Apart from Ottoman artists, there are also numerous sultans' portraits done by European painters. These Western painters would do their portraits based either on miniatures, early engravings, or on their own

imaginations, depicting the sultans in a manner suitable to the European image of the Ottomans. There were, however, some painters who came as part of the retinue of travelers or ambassadors to the Ottoman lands and these painters had the opportunity to see the sultans at close range. Whether during the ceremony of paying the trimonthly stipend to the sultan's household soldiers, the Friday service, or various other ceremonies such as holiday festivities. This allowed them to paint more realistic portraits of the sultans.

As mentioned above, the first Ottoman sultan to actually pose for his portrait was Sultan Mehmed II; those portraits of him that are done according to the miniatures tradition are currently a part of the palace's manuscripts collection, while oil paintings of him are in the paintings collection. The oil painting of Mehmed II done by the palace painter Fausto Zonaro on the order of Sultan Abdülhamid II in 1907 is one of the collection's most important pieces; it is a copy of the portrait of Mehmed II done in 1480 by the famed Italian painter Gentile Bellini who the sultan had invited to the palace. Mehmed is known to have personally posed for Bellini's painting (currently housed in the National Gallery in London) which is why it is such a realistic depiction of the sultan's facial features.

The tradition of depicting the Ottoman dynasty as a whole in a single picture began in the time of Sultan Murad III (r. 1574-95) and gave a

Portrait of Sultan Mehmed II (1441-1446/1451-1481)
Fausto Zonaro, 1907

new direction and impetus to the development of sultan portraiture. The first historical text to thus depict the Ottoman sultans as a group-a genre known as "şemâilnâme" or "book of characteristics"-was the "Kıyâfetü'l-insâniye fî şemâ'ilü'l-Osmâniye" (Human Characteristics in the Characteristics of the Ottomans), prepared in the second half of the 16th century. The aim in the preparation of this work was to show the sultans therein depicted in a realistic and true-to-life manner. With this aim in mind, the Grand Vizier Sokollu Mehmed Pasha ordered a series of oil portraits from the famed contemporary Italian artist Veronese. This series of oil paintings of the Ottoman rulers from Osman I (r. 1299-1324) to Murad III (r. 1574-95) was made in Veronese's workshop following an examination

Portrait of the aged Sultan Suleiman the Magnificent, Veronese' workshop. Late 16th century

of historical texts and of European depictions of Ottoman sultans done up to that time. The series is currently housed in the Alte Pinakothek collection in Munich. Another copy of the series, also made in Veronese's workshop in the 16th century, is currently a part of the Topkapı Palace collection.

Among the collection's portraits of sultans done by Western painters is a group of four portraits dating to the 17th century that show a very different view. These portraits of Mehmed I (r. 1413-21), Murad II (r. 1421-41, 1446-51), Mustafa I (r. 1617-18, 1622-23) and Murad IV (r. 1623-40) are done on a fabric whose designs are Spanish, giving rise to the idea that they may have been done by a painter of Spanish origin.

△ *Sultan Murad IV (1623-1640) Portrait representing the sultan's youth. It is thought to have been painted by a painter of Spanish origin*

◁ *Portrait of Sultan Abdülhamid I by the palace painter Rafael or the Rafael school, 1757-1789*

Portrait Sultan Selim III, Andrea Appiant, 1807

In the early 18th century, the influence of Western painting in such areas as light and shade and perspective began to appear in the works of Ottoman miniaturists like Levnî, Abdullah Buhârî and Ali Üsküdarî while the transition from miniature painting to painting on canvas occurred in the second half of that century. The earliest examples of large oil portraits in the collection are the portraits of Sultan Mahmud I (r. 1730-54), Sultan Mustafa III (r. 1757-74) and Sultan Abdülhamid I (r.1774-89), all attributed to the palace painter Rafael. The move of Ottoman art from books to canvas is perhaps best represented by two identical portraits of Mustafa III, one executed on paper and the other on canvas.

Portrait of Sultan Osman I (1299-1326) by palace painter Konstantin Kapıdağlı, 1804-1806

One other Ottoman painter who helped shape pictorial art in the second half of the 18th century was Konstantin Kapıdağlı. Known chiefly as a portraitist, his paintings of Sultan Selim III (r. 1789-1807) are among the collection's most important examples of art reflecting contemporary portrait tradition. In the painting signed Resm-i Konstantin Kapıdağlı (Painting by Konstantin Kapıdağlı) and dated 1218 (1803 in the Gregorian calendar), the artist depicts the sultan seated in an interior with a rosary in his hand; in this work, Kapıdağlı has clearly distanced himself from the miniature tradition and the accustomed iconography of sultanic portraiture.

Another of Konstantin Kapıdağlı's most important works in the collection is his series of 28 portraits of the Ottoman sultans, commissioned by Selim III and done in gouache on paper between 1804 and 1806. With these portraits- rendered as engravings in 1815 (during the reign of Sultan Mahmud II) by John Young in London, where they were published as an album. Kapıdağlı brought a new understanding to the art of sultanic portraiture: as in the portraits European monarchs, the sultans were here shown standing, half-length and in three-quarter or full frontal profile with highly natural facial expressions. Below each portrait is depicted the accompanying sultan's victories, conquests or important building commissions. Having become widely known following their printing in an engraved version, Kapıdağlı's portraits became the model for 19th-century portraits of monarchs and genealogical bust portraits both in the Ottoman Empire and in Europe.

Genealogical portraits are another genre of sultanic portraiture found in the palace collection. In this genre, whose first examples were done in the time of Sultan Abdülhamid I (r. 1774-89), the portraits of the sultans are found within medallions situated on the branches of a tree; the medallions are connected to one another via branches or ribbons in such a way as to depict each sultan's lineage.

Sultan Selim III in his room (1789-1807). Court painter Konstantin Kapıdağlı, 1803

Genealogical tree of the Ottoman Sultans. Anonymous, 1866-67

Although the majority of the genealogical portraits made through the second half of the 19th century were anonymous, the Ottoman and Greek texts found on the paintings indicate that they were done by local Istanbul artists.

Beginning in the second half of the 18th century, when albums of paintings and engravings became rather widespread, Western painters coming to the empire in the retinues of British, Swedish, Italian, and particularly French ambassadors, on the invitation of the Ottoman palace, or as independent travelers painted portraits of the sultans in great numbers. The rise of the

Sultan Abdülmecid (1839-1861) David Wilkie, 1840

orientalist style in the 19th century led to an increase in Western painters' interest in Istanbul and in Ottoman life and so the tradition of sultanic portraiture continued during this period as well. Examples from this period housed in the palace collection include Italian painter Fausto Zonaro's portrait of Sultan Mehmed II, British painter Sir David Wilkie's portrait of Sultan Abdülmecid, Polish painter Stanislaw Chlebowski's portrait of Sultan Abdülaziz, Wilhelm Reuter's portrait of Sultan Mahmud II and Russian-Armenian painter Ivan Aivazovsky's portrait of Sultan Murad V. Portraits of sultans done on ivory and known as Imperial Depiction (Tasvîr-i Hümâyûn) were another type of portraiture to emerge in the 19th century, beginning in the time of Sultan Mahmud II (r. 1808-39) and continuing until the first half of the 20th century. Among the Ottoman artists who did work in the Imperial Depiction style were Sebuh Manas, Marras, Abdullah, and Antranik.

△ *The ivory portrait of Sultan Abdulaziz. Sebuh Menas, 1869*

◁ *Sultan Mahmud II (1808-1839) It is thought to have been painted by Wilhelm Reuter at the end of the 19th century*

Besides the palace collection's portraits of sultans, there are also portraits of the sultans' daughters and wives, of the princes, and of the Mughal emperors of India as well as portraits of intellectuals of the republican period. Additionally, among the portraits of the sultans are found engravings, oil paintings, watercolours, and lithographs of Istanbul done by Western artists who visited the city in the 18th and 19th centuries.

THE SURROUNDINGS OF THE TOPKAPI PALACE MUSEUM

HAGIA SOPHIA
Tel: +90 212 522 17 50
Sultanahmet Square/Istanbul

Hagia Sophia is one of the cardinal edifices in the history of world architecture. This edifice, which is included in the Unesco Cultural Heritage list, was turned into a mosque after Istanbul's conquest and into a museum upon the order of Atatürk in 1935. Hagia Sophia, meaning "holy wisdom", was built in five years upon the order of the Byzantine emperor Justinian I. The church was completed and sanctified on December 27th, 537. Hagia Sophia, the seat of the Patriarch of Constantinople and the focal point of the Eastern Orthodox Church under Byzantine rule, was designed by two architects, Isidore of Miletus and Anthemius of Tralles.

It is related that 10000 workmen were employed in the construction of Hagia Sophia. In 1453, when the Ottoman Sultan Mehmed II conquered Istanbul, the church was converted into a mosque. Mehmed II the Conqueror only had the figurative mosaics plastered over with a thin layer. Thanks to the Sultan's foresight, the mosaics hidden under plaster were preserved for centuries. After the Republic of Turkey was founded, the mosque was transformed into a museum by Atatürk's initiative and some of the plaster was removed in order to uncover the mosaics.

In the courtyard leading to the entrance of the Museum of Hagia Sophia are today found tombs from the Ottoman Era, the Primary School, and the Abolition Fountain.

On the other hand, in the first courtyard of the Topkapı Palace is found Hagia Irene, one of the oldest temples of Christianity. This edifice is a must-see, especially during music festivals and cultural events.

An average of 300 thousand people visit the Hagia Sophia Museum every day during summer months.

The museum is closed on Mondays.

THE BASILICA CISTERN
Tel: +90 212 522 12 59
Sultanahmet/İstanbul

The Basilica Cistern, located at the Sultanahmet Square, was built in 542, during the reign of Byzantine emperor Justinian I, in order to serve as a reservoir providing the palace with water. The cistern, called the Sunken Palace by the Ottomans, is 143 meters in length and 65 meters in width and covers an area of 9800 square meters. Today, the Basilica Cistern is a hub for a variety of cultural activities.

The cistern is open to visitors every day.

THE TURKISH AND ISLAMIC ARTS MUSEUM (Ibrahim Pasha Palace)
Tel: +90 212 518 18 05
Sultanahmet Square/İstanbul

The Turkish and Islamic Arts Museum is a major art museum with its highly significant and distinctive collections of Turkish and

Islamic arts. The Ibrahim Pasha Palace, which is one of the most salient examples of the Ottoman civil architecture of the 16th century, was built atop the foundations of the seats of the ancient Roman hippodrome. The palace was given by Suleiman the Magnificent to his Grand Vizier, Ibrahim Pasha as a gift in the 16th century.

The Turkish and Islamic Arts Museum has been awarded with the Special Jury Award of the Museum of the Year Competition of the European Council in 1984. This museum, which certainly ranks among the few, most important museums of the world in its domain, houses more than forty thousand works of art from almost every period of the history of Islamic arts, including carpets, manuscripts, stoneware, woodenware, chinaware, bronze art, priceless belts embellished with gems, and other exquisite artworks of high ethnographic value.

The museum is closed on Mondays.

THE SULTAN AHMED COMPLEX AND MOSQUE
Sultanahmet Square/İstanbul

The Sultan Ahmed Complex is located at the Sultanahmet Square, and faces the Hagia Sophia Mosque. It was built by Sedefkar Mehmed Ağa upon the order of Sultan Ahmed I. The mosque, whose structure is highly characteristic of 17th century architecture, is popularly known as the "Blue Mosque" for the blue ceramic tiles-the number of these tiles exceeds 20000-adorning the walls of its interior. This mosque owes its beauty not only to these priceless ceramic tiles, but also to its richly decorated minber inlaid with mother-of-pearl, its mihrab made of finely carved and sculptured marble, marvelous calligraphic inscriptions, wooden door inlaid with mother-of-pearl, windows and Koran reading stands.

The mosque is open every day. (During prayer services, you can walk around outside the mosque)

THE ARCHAEOLOGY MUSEUM
Tel: +90 212 520 77 42
The first courtyard of the Topkapı Palace
Sultanahmet-Gülhane Park/İstanbul

The Directorate of Istanbul Archeology Museums, functioning as a sub-branch of the General Directorate of Monuments and Museums of the Ministry of Culture of the Republic of Turkey, is located in the Sultanahmet district, on the right of the entrance of the Gülhane Park. The Istanbul Archeology Museum was established towards the end of the 19th century by the famous painter and museum director Osman Hamdi Bey as the Empire Museum and opened to public in 1891. The museum's collections consist of numerous priceless subterranean and above ground artifacts belonging to the various civilizations that had once inhabited Ottoman soil.

The Archeology Museum also houses the Old Eastern Works Museum containing artifacts from

Mesopotamia, as well as the Enameled Kiosk Museums, where Seljuk and Ottoman chinaware are exhibited. In the Old Eastern Work Museum, there is a "tablet archive" consisting of 75000 documents with cuneiform inscriptions.

The museum is closed on Mondays.

THE GREAT PALACE MOSAIC MUSEUM

Tel: +90 212 528 45 00
Arasta Bazaar,
Sultanahmet/İstanbul

The Great Palace Mosaic Museum was inaugurated as a branch of the Istanbul Archeology Museums in 1953 and later, in 1979, it was linked to the Hagia Sophia Museum. It is located on the south of the Sultan Ahmed Mosque, inside the Arasta Bazaar in the mosque's complex. The museum was constructed in such a manner that the surviving mosaic floor on the northeast of the Byzantine Great Palace's cloister was incorporated with the museum. The mosaics found in the Great Palace, dating back to A.D. 6th century, are examples of unequaled mastery.

The museum is closed on Wednesdays.

THE SULTANAHMET SQUARE (HIPPODROME)

The Sultanahmet Square is one of the principal squares of Istanbul. It was referred to as the Hippodrome during the Byzantine Era, and Horse Square during the Ottoman Era. The most important Byzantine edifices, whose remains have survived until today, were constructed around the Hippodrome. The imperial palace known as the Great Palace used to lie between the Hippodrome and the Sea of Marmara.

The most precious edifices of the city of Istanbul, such as Hagia Sophia, the Sultan Ahmed Mosque, The Turkish and Islamic Arts Museum and the Basilica Cistern are located in the vicinity of the Hippodrome.

This square was also the scene for the Nika riots in the Byzantine Era, and the Janissary riots. Besides, the ancient Egyptian Obelisk of Theodosius, the Serpent Column and the Walled Obelisk stand erect in this square.

With these matchless monuments, the Horse Square or the Hippodrome, remains the major touristic hub of Istanbul.

The German Fountain, a gift from the German Emperor Wilhelm II to the Sultan and to his city, faces the tomb of Sultan Ahmed I and the Hagia Sophia Museum.

The Bath of Roxelana, constructed in the 16th century by the famous Ottoman architect Sinan in the name of Suleiman the Magnificent's wife Haseki Hürrem Sultan is also in the Sultanahmet Square. This edifice hosts various cultural events today.

SOĞUK ÇEŞME SOKAĞI (Literally: Street of the Cold Fountain)

Soğuk çeşme Sokağı, which lies between Hagia Sophia and the Topkapı Palace in the district of Sultanahmet, is a pedestrian

Hagia Sophia in 537. The church underwent several renovations as it was damaged by earthquakes and fires in the subsequent centuries. The current building largely reflects the reconstruction following the earthquake of 740. Hagia Irene served as an armoury and a military museum during the Ottoman period.

Today the church is a museum, requiring special permission for admission. However, it is one of the most popular concert halls of the Istanbul International Music Festival because of its acoustic properties.

BEYAZIT MOSQUE

Beyazit Mosque is located on the European side of Istanbul,in Beyazit Square which is situated in Eminonu district. Constraction of the mosque started in 1500 and ended in 1505. The architect of Beyazit Mosque is not excactly known. It can be Architect Hayrettin,Architect Kemalettin or Yakupsah bin Sultansah.Beyazit Mosque compelx consists of many parts, such as mosque, medrese, bath, kitchen...

THE FOUNTAIN OF SULTAN AHMED III

The Fountain of Sultan Ahmed III is located at the great square in front of the Imperial Gate of Topkapı Palace. It is a Rococo edifice that was built under Sultan Ahmed III in 1728, in the style of the Tulip period. It was a social centre and gathering place.

NURUOSMANIYE MOSQUE

Nuruosmaniye Mosque meaning "The Light of Osman" was first constructed by Sultan Mahmud I in 1748 and was completed during Sultan Osman III reign in 1755. It was built on top of one of the seven hills of Istanbul by two architects: Greek architect named Simeon and Mustafa Aga.

THE SULEYMANIYE MOSQUE

The Suleymaniye Mosque is located on the Third Hill of Istanbul . It is considered the second largest mosque in the city . It was built between 1550-1557 AD by Sultan Suleyman the Magnificent who was the richest and most powerful Sultan of the Ottoman empire. It was designed by the great Ottoman architect Mimar Sinan.

ŞEHZADE MOSQUE

Sehzade Mosque is located on the third hill of Istanbul. It is also known as the "Prince's Mosque". It was built by Sultan Suleiman I in memory of his eldest son, Prince Mehmet, who died a sudden death at the age of 21 in 1543.

street along which wooden houses modeled upon Ottoman civil architecture are found. This street is named after a historical Turkish marble fountain dating back to 1800, to the reign of Selim III. The wooden houses along the street were restored by the Touring and Automobile Club and turned into pensions. On the other hand, this street houses the Istanbul Library and the cistern which has been converted into a restaurant.

THE ARASTA BAZAAR

This bazaar, also known as the Cavalry Bazaar, was constructed as the complement of the Sultan Ahmet Complex, so as to provide revenue to the complex. Today in this historical bazaar, which comprises a long street with shops on both sides, selling hand-woven antique carpets, silverware, and souvenirs made of felt.

THE GRAND BAZAAR

The Grand Bazaar, situated in the midst of Nuruosmaniye, Mercan, and Beyazıt, is the oldest and largest shopping center of the world, with its 64 streets and roads, two covered bazaars, 16 inns, 22 gates and about 3,600 shops. Nearly 20,000 people are employed in the bazaar, which covers an approximate area of 45,000 square meters. Depending on the season, it receives around 300 - 500 thousand local and foreign visitors a day.

The bazaar is closed on Sundays, and during the Ramadan, the Festival of Sacrifice, and the Republic Day. During weekdays, it is open between 8:30 am and 7:00 pm.

THE ÇORLULU ALI PASHA MADRASAH
Tel: +90 212 519 23 41

Situated at the Divanyolu Caddesi in the vicinity of Çemberlitaş, The Çorlulu Ali Pasha Madrasah was constructed as a complex together with The Çorlulu Ali Pasha Mosque. It is the most popular place in Istanbul for nargileh smokers. One can hardly comprehend the historical significance of the peninsula without smoking nargileh in the traditional café inside this edifice woven with history. Among its frequenters are pensioners, local shopkeepers, and tourists. In the carpet shops, one can also receive repairment service and buy authentically-designed lanterns as souvenirs. The ambiance of the madrasah is tranquil and otherworldly. It is open to visitors between 7:00 am and 2:00 am.

THE CHURCH OF SAINT IRENE

The church of Saint Irene ("Holy Peace", Turkish " Aya İrini") is located in the first courtyard of the Topkapı Palace. Commissioned by Constantine I in the 4th century on the site of a temple dedicated to Venus, Saint Irene is one of the first churches of Constantinople. The original wooden structure was burnt down during the Nika revolt in 532, to be renovated by Justinian I. Saint Irene served as the Patriarchal church before the completion of